KT-512-972

Clive Fisher is a journalist and reviewer for the
Catholic Herald.
He has also written for the Londoner's Diary and the
books page of the *Financial Times*. This is his first
book.

Also available from Futura
in this series

BEECHAM STORIES

COMPILED BY CLIVE FISHER

Gielgud Stories

Anecdotes, sayings and impressions of Sir John Gielgud

Futura

A Futura Book

ISBN 0 7088 3988 6

Typeset, printed and bound in Great Britain by
Hazell Watson & Viney Limited
Member of BPCC plc
Aylesbury, Bucks, England

Futura Publications
A Division of
Macdonald & Co (Publishers) Ltd
66–73 Shoe Lane
London EC4P 4AB
A member of Maxwell Pergamon Publishing Corporation plc

For Matthew Sturgis

Contents

Introduction

It was only after having collected most of the comments and stories which follow that I saw BEST OF FRIENDS at the Apollo Theatre this February. The production marked Sir John Gielgud's return to the theatre after a protracted absence spent largely in the studios of television and the cinema. It was the second time that I had seen Gielgud on stage: ten years ago, with an early schoolboyish enthusiasm for Shakespeare, I had come from the country to see the National Theatre's JULIUS CAESAR, with Sir John as the eponymous hero. When I embarked on this project, my memories of that occasion were indistinct: Caesar is not a part central to the play, either in length or thematic purpose; subsequent study of literature at school and university had changed beyond recognition my views about the interpretation of literature on stage; and besides, a decade is a long time.

What I saw earlier this year was, therefore, a revelation; to some extent also, a vindication of the fervent tribute which has been laid at this man's feet for the greater part of the twentieth century. Despite the fact that Sir John was undeniably ill at ease, nervous, forgetful of his lines and sometimes clumsy in his movements, his performance contained one thrilling aspect denied his fellow actors. In Gielgud's stage presence, most actors (including Rosemary Harris and Ray McAnally, his co-stars that evening) are put at a disadvantage by their delivery of lines. I do not refer to the fact that many actors have voices which, compared to Sir John's, are unmemorable. Instead, what struck me that evening, sitting towards the back of the circle, was the brilliance of his vocal control. Much of his part was soliloquy, that most challenging of stage disciplines—how to convey in a fashion at once audible and realistic the inner workings of the mind. Whereas most actors, mindful of their early training, consciously and obviously project to the back of the gallery, determined at all costs to be heard, Gielgud made an intimate chamber of the huge theatre and words written as whispered confidences and mumbled half-thoughts came across with seemingly effortless clarity. And I realized why, despite several outstanding film performances, Sir John belongs to the theatre and cinema can never appropriate him.

I became aware in my researches of another aspect of Gielgud's uniqueness. In the bitchy world of show business, with its fragile egos, its jealous competitiveness and the mocking promises it makes of success and fame, Sir John's popularity is absolute. Again and again, he has been praised not only for his genius, but also for his sympathy and generosity.

I have no particular debts of assistance or encouragement to declare. But I should like to take this opportunity to say how much I have enjoyed compiling this collection of stories. I hope you enjoy reading it.

Clive Fisher, 1988

Ideas About Acting

Sir John:
I do have a good figure, but I am inclined to walk so badly, the critics were quite right.

Sir John Mills:
Sir John Gielgud, not long ago, was questioned by a reporter on the subject of retirement. 'Sir John, you are over seventy, still playing long parts and acting them with your usual brilliance; if, God forbid, at some time in the let's hope long-distant future your memory begins to fail and you find it impossible to remember your lines, I suppose you will be forced reluctantly to retire.'

Sir John regarded the reporter with a slightly incredulous look on his face and replied, 'My dear fellow, there's always the radio!'

Sir John writes to the *Observer* on March 17th, 1935, concerning the future of the National Theatre:

Supposing the three institutions, Stratford, the Old Vic and Sadler's Wells were in a sense amalgamated, and endowed on a large scale as the genuine foundation of a National Theatre. In the first place, the companies would be interchangeable, and infinitely more care could be given to each production. A play could run for a month at the Old Vic, then go to Stratford, then to Sadler's Wells, and then perhaps to tour for a month. Having only to produce a new play every three or four months would give a producer much more time to put his best work into each . . . To my mind, the Old Vic, subsidized and linked with Stratford-upon-Avon, has the best claims to be made the basis of a really National Theatre. If rebuilding there is to be—and I suppose its own building would be demolished when the great South of the River Embankment Scheme comes off—then what more suitable than that it should arise, phoenix-like, from its own ashes, on its old site, or near its own site, as the corner-stone of the scheme.

◊

Sir John:

At drama school I had loved trailing my black cloak around, posing and being emotional, but I had a feeling there was something wrong with that.

◊

Sir John:

The first time I saw my name in lights was in 1928 in a farce with Hermione Baddeley. It was an appalling concoction, backed by the lady who had written it, called *Holding Out the Apple*. It contained, among many others, one immortal line: 'You've got a way of holding out the apple that positively gives me the pip.' It ran about six weeks, largely to an audience of nurses in free seats.

◊

Judi Dench:
You don't get a letter if he hasn't been happy with the production or your performance. We knew, during one night of *Antony and Cleopatra,* that he was in the audience. A couple of days later, Tony (Hopkins) said, 'Did you hear from John?' And I said, 'Uhm . . . no. Did you?' He said, 'Uhm . . . no.' A few days later, I saw Peter (Hall). He said, 'Er . . . did you get a letter from John?' I said, 'No, did you?' After a pause, he said, 'No'. And then quite suddenly three arrived the next day. They'd just taken time to write, I suppose. But the sense of relief was definitely there. I've got a lot of those letters and they're incredibly difficult to read. But what he says is what he thinks and you won't get a letter if he didn't like it.

◊

Sir John on style:
Knowing which play you're in.

◊

Sir John:
For a long time, my ambition was to be frightfully smart and West End, wear beautifully-cut suits lounging on sofas in french window comedies.

◊

Emlyn Williams:
A friend told me of an example of John's absorption

13

in the theatre, which cropped up quite unexpectedly. The two of them, playing in the same film, were sitting on the set in their canvas chairs, whiling away one of the long waits; John was reading. The other, wrestling with his *Times* crossword, leant over, 'Sorry, but is there a character in Shakespeare called the Earl of Westmoreland?'

'Yes,' John answered, without looking up, 'in *Henry IV Part Two*.' Then, to break the bad news, he turned to my friend. 'But it's a very poor part.' And went back to his book.

◊

Sir John, recalling the distant days just before the war, when he was almost exclusively a classical actor:

In those days, except for *Musical Chairs*, I never seemed to be cast in modern dress except to play prigs or bores.

◊

And modern dress or no, *Musical Chairs* was not without incident, as Sir John again remembers:

Another evening I noticed Noel Coward in front. I recognized him immediately, became very nervous, and played the first act with one eye on him all the time. The curtain rose after the first interval, and I looked again in Noel's direction. He had not returned and his seat was empty for the rest of the performance. For the next few weeks I was very hurt and complained to my friends how rude he had been in walking out. At last I ran across him, and he said frankly, 'You were overacting so terribly that I couldn't have borne it another minute, and Frank Vosper's wig was so badly joined that it looked like a yachting-cap!' He also said (though not to me), that he would never have dreamed of leaving the

14

theatre had he known that his exit would be noticed. 'This incident,' he remarked, 'has finally convinced me that I am really famous.'

The same incident really broke me for good of my dreadful habit of looking at people in the audience.

ϙ

Alan Bennett receives some advice:

A lovely Gielgud remark: he asks me whether I couldn't write a Noel Coward parody for the second act (of *Forty Years On*):

'You know the sort of thing, lots of little epigrams, smart witty remarks. It wouldn't be at all difficult.'

'I couldn't possibly.'

'Why not? It's terribly easy. Noel does it all the time.'

ϙ

Sir John took over from Noel Coward the part of Nicky Lancaster in Coward's *The Vortex*. He cannot have been an easy act to follow:

We were acting at the Little Theatre in John Street, Adelphi one night, when a cat came on to the stage while we were playing the big emotional scene in the last act. I became so hysterical that I threw it into the audience. Fortunately the auditorium was almost level with the stage, and the cat was able to slip away.

ϙ

Musical Chairs, once again. And the audience continues to be as distinguished as the cast. Sir John:

My impromptu piano-playing in the part served well enough, but I became self-conscious about that too after a while, especially one night when I saw Arthur Rubinstein sitting in the second row of the stalls.

15

Sir John Gielgud:
I find it practically impossible to be disliked on stage.

♀

Sir Peter Hall recalls a rehearsal for *The Tempest* in which Gielgud played Prospero:
John talked to me afterwards with the kind of modesty and frankness which make him a great man. He said he knew that in some senses he had become old-fashioned—all actors do. He remembered in his youth how wonderfully immediate Balliol Holloway and Dorothy Green had been—the new actors of that age. Yet, by the end of their lives, even they seemed to him rhetorical old hams. He felt he was the same, which is why he wanted to do *The Tempest* the way I wanted. And, said he, the stage always went to his head anyway. He loved to wander around swinging his cloak and dominating the audience. It was a romantic style of acting which had served him well all his life and his public loved it. But, added John, I want to get rid of my easy solutions.

♀

Sir John:
I was sixteen by now and very vain. I affected very light grey flannels braced much too high, silk socks, broad-brimmed black soft hats, and even, I blush to admit it, an eye-glass upon occasion, and I wore my hair very long and washed it a great deal to make it look fluffy and romantic. For Orlando (in *As You Like It*), I slipped off to a hairdresser in St Leonards and asked the man to wave it—'For a play,' I added hastily. 'Certainly, sir,' he said. 'I suppose you'd be in the Variety Company that's opening on the Pier this week.'

16

Sir John:

I think perhaps the only really original contribution that I have made to the history of the part has been to play it successfully when I was younger than most Hamlets have been allowed to do.

◊

Gielgud went on tour with his swansong production of *Hamlet* just after the war. Donald Sinden encountered him in Bombay:

John and I were walking along the coast and with all the innocence of youth I asked him what he considered the most important elements of acting. He thought for a second and replied, 'I should say *feeling* and *timing*,' and then he flashed me a look out of the corner of his eyes and gurgled, 'I understand it's the same in many walks of life.'

◊

Sir John:

I was highly amused by a comment Bernard Shaw made once in a letter to Edith Evans, when we were playing together in *The Seagull* and Shaw refused to admit that I was any good at all. Indeed, he thought my performance was so dreadful that the play was ruined every time I came on the stage. I suppose he had no idea that I had a Lithuanian background on my father's side which might have given me an insight into Russian plays and literature. 'Of course,' he wrote, 'John Gielgud, although he can be very good when he is rightly cast, couldn't possibly play anything by Chekhov, being a Terry.'

◊

Sir John:
With the Shakespeare parts I learned how to project a performance and with the Chekhov parts I learned how not to project it.

ç

Sir Peter Hall:
I wandered about giving stray *Volpone* notes to any actors I could find before the play's first preview tonight. John Gielgud wants to re-focus his performance and make it realer. So . . . Sir John rehearsed. In the middle of it all I mentioned something to do with over-playing. He blushed and said, 'Will I never learn? Still my old tricks after years and years and years: anything for a laugh, and because of that I don't get it.'

ç

Alan Bennett:
In the morning the plotting (for *Forty Years On*) goes ahead slowly, with Gielgud sitting apart doing his eternal crossword. I have heard stories that he is apt to fill in any old word that is the right length. I sneak a look and am disappointed to find this a myth. He learns his script by writing it out in a neat hand on the page opposite the text. 'I am a very bad study. After fifty, one gets much worse.'

ç

Charles Sturridge:
On the Saturday after Olivier left, I went down to Oxfordshire and then drove up to Yorkshire with John Gielgud. We were shooting (for *Brideshead Revisited*) at Castle Howard, so that four or five hour journey was our first meeting. I was absolutely terrified. But it was

a wonderful experience. He'd just been doing his auto-biography on the radio. He was very conversant with his life and I think he had just finished a book as well. So we were sitting in this very grand car provided by the studio to get us from Aylesbury to York. He told me to recount my life story. That occupied the first fifteen minutes or so. Then he spoke for the remaining four or five hours, giving a breathtaking, thrilling account of his life. He had a terrifyingly accurate power of recall. For someone who can't remember what he was doing last Tuesday, he would be talking about Saturday after-noon matinées in 1934. All one had to do was listen. He was a perfect companion, a wonderful raconteur and word-perfect in the part of his own life story.

◊

Sir Alec Guinness remembers first working with Sir John in the latter's production of *Hamlet*:

It was after a week of rehearsing that he spoke 'spon-taneously' to me, with shattering effect. 'What's hap-pened to you?' he cried. 'I thought you were rather good. You're terrible. Oh, go away! I don't want to see you again!'

I hung around at rehearsal until the end of the day and then approached him cautiously. 'Excuse me, Mr Gielgud, but am I fired?' 'No! Yes! No, of course not. But go away. Come back in a week. Get someone to teach you how to act. Try Martita Hunt; she'll be glad of the money.'

◊

Judi Dench:

John once said to me, 'Isn't it awful? After a perform-ance, I'm so nervous, people come into my room and

19

they don't say anything and I ask them questions and then answer them myself.'

Apparently, on one occasion after a performance in Stratford he heard Patience Collyer coming along the corridor—he and Patience were great friends—and he went out through the window and climbed over the balcony!

◊

Sir John:
I am very keen on pace, and I always think it is frightfully important to ensure the audience is not bored and that they do not fall asleep or leave the theatre. Shaw always said, 'speak to the lines and with the lines but never in between the lines.'

◊

Judi Dench:
I remember his once saying to me, 'Even if the stage doorman tells me he doesn't like the colour of my shoes for a play I'll worry about it. And if someone says before a play, "I don't think you should wear brown shoes, I think you should wear black," and someone else says, "I don't think you should wear black shoes, I think you should wear brown," I would probably go on wearing one of each colour.'

◊

Judi Dench:
He came to *Macbeth* when we did it at the Other Place and said afterwards that he thought all those great tragic vehicles should be done in a space like that so that you don't have to over-project them, so that you can do them incredibly intensely.

Sir John:
Acting is half shame, half glory. Shame at exhibiting yourself, glory when you can forget yourself.

◊

Peter Brook:
John's highly developed sense of responsibility to an audience is greater than his responsibility to himself, and so, of the two integrities, John, unlike a number of actors, will sacrifice not only himself but the reality of his own work for the sake of not letting the audience down . . . a director can help by concentrating on him in a way that he won't concentrate on himself, creating for him a climate of selfishness that he won't create for himself . . . Submerged in each one of John's perform-ances is a core which is pure, clear, strong, simple and utterly realistic. The act of working rightly is, for him, to come towards that core.

◊

His first drama teacher's assessment:
He walked like a cat with rickets.

◊

Michael Feast:
I learned about verse speaking and metre and breathing from Sir John . . . I also learned a vitally important lesson from Gielgud and one that I have only really in the last five years benefited from. And that is how to pace oneself, conserve one's energy and how to look after one's body, mind and soul, not just in performance but throughout the whole process and cycle of rehearsal and playing. Sir John takes great care of himself and I don't feel that that is something

he has just come to in later age. I think that he has evolved it over the years and it is a very important aspect of being an actor in this strange and somewhat psychically disruptive business.

◊

As a drama student desperately in need of a job, Sir Alec Guiness applied to Gielgud, then at Wyndham's Theatre in *The Maitlands*. After unsuccessfully attending two auditions Sir John had recommended, Guinness returned to report on his progress:

When I went back to Wyndham's that evening I had only fourpence left in the world and during the last two days had eaten two buns, two apples and had a couple of glasses of milk. John looked at me gravely when I told him of my Old Vic experience and then said, 'I believe in you. But you are far too thin. You're not eating enough.' On his make-up table was a pile of crisp pound notes. 'Here's twenty pounds,' he said, 'until I can give you a job.' He must have had the gesture in mind and tried to hand me the money. Perhaps I was just too proud to accept, and rather light-headed from want of food, but twenty pounds was quite a sum in those days and I was terrified of getting into debt. Rather grandly, and certainly foolishly, I assured him I had no need of money . . .

Several weeks later I went to a matinee at the Old Vic (of *Richard II*, with Maurice Evans) and, seated in the pit, glimpsed Gielgud in the front stalls. In an interval I followed him to the coffee bar, not with the intention of speaking to him but just to be in his presence. He suddenly spotted me and came over, saying, 'Where have you been? I've made enquiries for you all over London. I want you to play Osric in *Hamlet*. Rehearsals start on Monday week at the New Theatre.' . . . My joy was almost out of control when I heard my salary in *Hamlet* would be seven pounds a week. But I hadn't foreseen the agony of rehearsals.

◊

Sir Peter Hall experienced Gielgud's generosity many years later:

Buffet supper on the terraces of John Gielgud's home in the country. It is now finished and very beautiful, but a little like living in the William and Mary wing of the Victoria and Albert Museum: decorated out of its life and rather impersonal; exquisite taste though. A happy paradox: there is John standing in the middle of his palace, the wonderful salmon and chilled white wine spread out in the background, and saying mournfully that he's broke and can't even write a cheque. He looks as if he should be wearing a full-bottomed wig.

◊

Derek Granger:

While I was dining with him in Manchester, just before the last bout of filming on *Brideshead*, he explained how much of his life, during breaks from work, was now spent with music and books, reading, playing the gramophone and enjoying the simple and peaceful pleasures of country life. I remonstrated with him over the fact that his friends complained they never saw him, that people were saying he had become reclusive, that he was impossible to get hold of, that he hardly ever went out.

'Oh,' he replied. 'But I've been out.'

◊

Sir John:

I am a born Cockney, and as soon as I was given a latch-key and allowed to go out alone I used to walk about the London streets all day long.

◊

Sir Peter Hall again:

John said how wonderful it was to have a free after-noon in London. He isn't really enjoying the country, I think: he's a town rat, as Ralph (Richardson) has always observed.

◊

Richard Clowes:

The nearest John's ever got to politics is the plot of *Julius Caesar*.

◊

Beverley Nichols recalls Gielgud's arriving to stay on the eve of war:

He arrived on an evening of acute international tension. We were sitting round in a state of unaccustomed gloom, wondering what was going to happen to us all, whether we should be able to finish our books or our poems or our paintings or our music, or whether we were all going to be swept up in the approaching holocaust. 'If you're all so worried about what's going to happen,' said John, 'why don't you turn on the radio?' 'There isn't one,' I said. 'That,' replied John, 'is excellent news, because I shall be able to listen to myself talking . . .' And talk he did, brilliantly, till the small hours of the morning—not about Hitler or Mussolini or any of the other ogres who were haunting us, but about the theatre, which was all he knew about or thought important in this distracted world.

On the following morning I rose early, to get the papers from the village post office. But I found that John had forestalled me. He was sitting in the music room, surrounded by scattered copies of the Sunday papers, whose headlines were double-decked with disaster. Ultimatums, troop movements, diplomatic scurryings, mobilizations. His face was dark.

'What in heaven's name has happened?' I demanded.

His face grew darker. But he had not noticed the headlines. He was scanning the theatrical pages.

'The worst,' he proclaimed in sepulchral tones. 'Gladys has got the most appalling notices. And so has the play.' He strode to the window and stared out. 'I don't know what the world is coming to.'

◊

Sir John:

I have three besetting sins, both on and off the stage—impetuosity, self-consciousness, and a lack of interest in anything not immediately concerned with myself or with the theatre.

◊

Sir Alec Guinness:

It was at the lunch in York, I remember, that a waitress asked him to sign the tablecloth. 'I'm sure she doesn't know me from Adam,' he said. 'She'll be terribly disappointed if I put my own name.' So he signed 'Jack Buchanan', and the waitress was thrilled.

◊

Some are more easily impressed than others, however. Sir John again:

The Vic was about to open again for a new season (in 1934) and Lilian (Baylis, the Vic's manager) sent me one

25

of her characteristic letters (neatly typed, with most of the typing crossed out and her own writing crowded in on top of it) asking me to come down to see her and discuss some of her plans. Delighted and flattered at being considered so important, I stepped into my car and drove to the Vic. I marched into Lilian's office in my best West End style, with new hat and yellow gloves held negligently in my hand. Lilian greeted me warmly and we talked enthusiastically together for half an hour. As I got up to go I said grandly, 'I should simply love to come some time and act and direct again at the Vic for you if you'd let me, but of course I'm awfully busy for the next month or two.' Lilian, looking steadily at my rapidly receding hair, said briskly, 'Oh no, dear, you play all the young parts you can while you're still able to!' I left the Vic in a distinctly chastened frame of mind, determined that I would never again attempt to impress so shrewd a judge of character as Lilian Baylis.

◊

Some of Sir John's friends were rather less subtle in their references to his receding hair. Emlyn Williams went to discuss his play, *Spring, 1600*, with Gielgud in 1933:

The door was opened by my old friend Richard Clowes ... Dick introduced me to John Perry, who shared the flat ... Dick asked if John Gielgud was still asleep.

'He's in the bathroom massaging the old temples. I keep telling him it's no use playing Canute, we'll both be bald by forty.'

◊

Sir John:
I am not clever at drawing people out, and my friends

26

tell me that I have no real interest in anyone but myself. I hope this is not the exact truth.

◊

Peter Ustinov appeared with Gielgud in *Crime and Punishment* in 1945:

John Gielgud is so contorted with shyness at first meetings that he makes a normally shy person like myself feel brash, and even boorish. And yet, despite this gossamer delicacy, there are heights to rise to before an anonymous public, and an ego, totally invisible in the drawing-room, imperceptibly takes over. As the curtain fell in the first act of *Crime and Punishment* during the first performance, he suddenly trumpeted a message to us all. 'If there are going to have to be all these people in the wings, they must look at me!' He found it impossible to play to backs turned in discretion, in order not to break his concentration. To hell with the concentration, once there were people he was hungry for faces!

◊

Sir John was asked by Emlyn Williams and his wife to be the godfather to their son:

Not really my part, my dears, but I'll have a shot at it . . .

◊

The memorial services of Marie Rambert and Kenneth More followed each other in quick succession. Such occasions are not always uplifting.

Gielgud:

Sometimes, I feel as if I may as well stay on for my own.

◊

Sir Alec Guinness:
Gielgud is a workaholic, even in his eighties.

ζ

Stanley Kauffman:
Gielgud has become proof, irrefutable, that he thought of his life in relation to artistic purpose—with art as his centripetal force, his map, his reason for getting through each day and wanting to get up again next morning. Only an artist who gets serious joy out of shaping his life to nourish his art can finish like Gielgud.

ζ

Sir John reflects that some of the lessons of one's schooldays are lessons learnt for life:
My talent for games remained at zero, but I somehow managed to get into the Second XI at football. When a notice was put up at end of the term assessing the merits of each individual member of the team, my name was at the bottom with the remark: 'Gielgud. An opportunist merely.' I have always tried to live up to this.

ζ

Edward Fox:
To me, Gielgud is simply a great actor and a great man, whose life's work is an example and a lesson that all we, who work in the theatre, should pay heed to with the most profound respect, daily and on our knees!

ζ

The adoration has been going on for a long time. Lord Olivier recalls his first collaboration with Gielgud, in *Romeo and Juliet*, in 1934:

He was giving the familiar tradition fresh life, whereas I was completely disregarding the old in favour of something new. Somehow I feel that he was a little led by the nose by his audience and by his acolytes. He was greatly admired, in fact adored, and like all of us at some time in our careers he believed his publicity. So, by the time we did *Romeo*, I was considered by the Establishment to be against him. Everybody was in his favour, while I was on another planet.

◊

Sir John discussing *Othello* with Dame Peggy Ashcroft:

'I don't really know what jealousy is,' he said. Then he caught himself. 'Oh, yes, I do! I remember! When Larry (Olivier) had a success as *Hamlet*, I wept.'

◊

Judi Dench:

Somebody told me that he went to receive some order or other. Apparently he did nothing but complain to the Queen. He did nothing throughout the entire audience but complain to the Queen that he couldn't possibly afford to stay in this country because of the tax! He is blazingly honest.

◊

Charles Dance:

One of my ambitions is to reach the grand age of eighty-three and be able to act as well as he does and to be as much in demand as he is.

◊

Judi Dench:
John has a very strange way of looking at you on stage. He'll glance at you and then look at you always to one side of your face.

 ♩

Sir John:
Even today I still weep so easily at a play that I am sometimes ashamed of myself. The Terrys all have the same weakness, on and off the stage. 'Weak lachrymal glands, my dear,' said a famous specialist to my mother, who was particularly afflicted in this way. This capacity for crying easily is sometimes useful to me as an actor, and the sight of real tears always impresses those in an audience who are sitting close enough to see them. But on some nights the tears refuse to come, and then I feel I am not giving my best at that particular performance. Fortunately, however, the effect is more important than the tears themselves, which actually convince the actor more than the audience. I remember being much impressed by hearing my cousin, Phyllis Neilson-Terry, say one night . . . 'Shall I give them them real tears tonight?' . . . Ellen Terry says in her book, 'My real tears on the stage astonished some people, and have been the envy of others, but they have often been a hindrance to me. I have had to work to restrain them.'

 ♩

Judi Dench:
He and Peggy came to *A Midsummer Night's Dream* when we did it at Stratford. The next day I got the most enormous bouquet of every white flower you can imagine. John's message was, 'I felt I could fly away with you.'

Peter Brook:
John is always in the present; he is modern in his restless quest for truth and new meaning. He is also traditional, for his passionate sense of quality comes from his understanding of the past. He links two ages. He is unique.

♩

Judi Dench:
He gave me the most wonderful present on the first night of *Gay Lord Quex*, the most enormous shell you've ever seen, mounted on a stand. It had absolutely no significance at all; that's why I loved it.

♩

Charles Sturridge:
When we started shooting *Brideshead*, *Caligula* had just come out. The press immediately started baying for his blood, insisting that he stand up and announce that he had been tricked into playing pornography. But he refused and was quite happy to admit that he had been sent the script, that he had read it, taken a decision and was not ashamed of that decision. He is totally unembarrassed about *Caligula*, and utterly uncoy about sex and *refused* to be made to seem so!

♩

Judi Dench:
He once said to me that he likes going to the cinema better than the theatre because in a theatre he knows he's got to stay to the end, while in a cinema it's so dark that no one can see him sneak out.

Judi Dench:
I took him on my Desert Island in 1970 or so. I took him doing Seven Ages. I also took a pair of Wellington boots because I'm afraid of worms and all the films of Basil Brush, because I was besotted with Basil Brush. All the other choices would be different now, except John. I'd still take him.

◊

After *Richard of Bordeaux* and *Spring, 1600*, Gielgud starred in a contemporary play, *The Maitlands*, in 1934. Everything was done with good reason:
If my public don't see me soon in a pair of trousers, they'll think I haven't got any.

Before the Curtain Goes Up

The part of Prospero is one Sir John knows well. That familiarity can, however, be a hindrance when it comes to interpreting the character for yet another production. Sir Peter Hall recalls his adaptation of 1973:

John Gielgud began the afternoon by announcing that he didn't want to wear a beard or hat or be in grey or black as Prospero, who was a boring man, and it was a boring part, and he didn't want to look boring. He questioned practically everything that I proposed . . . John remembered that when he first played *The Tempest*, it was all divinely Eastern and he wore a turban. In a later production, he recalled, he wore a long grey beard and glasses. Then in Peter Brook's he had some kind of ragged, hermity shift with sandals. At the end of three hours, I had gently but firmly ridden John to a standstill and managed to get him to listen to why I was doing the play in a Jacobean masque-like way. He then announced that he loved the set, and perhaps he had better wear a buttoned, belted, scholar's coat after all. And a beard (should he grow it or have a false one?) And he agreed to wear a scholar's hat. John Gielgud runs around in circles with huge charm and energy. He keeps making self-deprecating remarks, reminding us we shouldn't listen to him, and that he is a romantic who loves the old-fashioned theatre.

◊

Sir John is celebrated for his fertility of invention when it comes to staging plays. Not all playwrights find his resourcefulness reassuring, however. Gielgud met T. S. Eliot to discuss *The Family Reunion*:

We had oysters, I remember, and it was very formal. I was rather nervous and began to draw patterns on the tablecloth. 'Should the set be like this?' I asked him. 'The French windows, should they be here?' and, 'How do you want the Eumenides to be seen? Or should they be invisible, or perhaps in masks?' The more I talked, the more silent Eliot became. However, I left thinking that I had created quite a good impression. I continued to think so until, a few days later, I met Sybil Thorndike who said, 'You know, Eliot's not going to let you have his play—he says you have no faith.' Evidently he feared I was going to turn it into a fashionable Shaftesbury Avenue comedy . . .

◊

Judi Dench:

We rehearsed *The Gay Lord Quex* under Saint James's Piccadilly. John kept changing all the time. He liked what I did at the beginning and so I went through a kind of hoop for him and he said, 'I think after all that you should go back to what you were doing at the beginning.' One morning, we were rehearsing there and quite suddenly there was a bang and out of the loo downstairs there ran a man or boy or whatever with a pair of trousers shrieking up the stairs and after him ran another man *without* any trousers! We laughed till we cried and John had to break rehearsals. Our minds raced but we never got to the bottom of it.

◊

Sir John and Sir Ralph were to be reunited in Enid Bagnold's *The Last Joke*. It had been the playwright's intention that the character to be played by Gielgud take poison. However, as Bagnold recalled, John Gielgud wanted to shoot himself. 'And amid fireworks . . . For so great, so beautiful, so perfect an actor he was being silly. Stars are sometimes silly, but very seldom he.'

◊

Kitty Black acted as a secretary to Binkie Beaumont, producer of a Gielgud adaptation of *Macbeth*:

For a long time John couldn't make up his mind about the Lady, and finally announced that he would hold auditions in order to find a suitable new star. Among the letters was one application for the part of 'Lady McBeth' enclosing a photograph with the pathetic P.S. 'I do take my glasses off often.' Eventually he settled for Gwen Ffrangcon-Davies who had been his exquisite partner in the romantic smash-hit, *Richard of Bordeaux*, as well as in *The Three Sisters* and *The Importance of Being Earnest*.

From the first the disasters that seem to dog the Scottish play began to accumulate. First, William Walton disappeared. His agent had no idea where he was and as the music he had been commissioned to write had been conceived as an accompaniment to all the witches' scenes, which were to be spoken rhythmically against a recorded score, nobody could rehearse anything final until the composer had set down what had been agreed with the director. One day the office boy came into my room saying: 'There's a bloke outside who says he's supposed to be composing the music for *Macbeth*.'

'Mr Walton, Mr Walton,' I cried, hurrying out to meet him, 'where have you been? Where is the music?'

'I haven't written it yet,' he replied.

'Not written it!' I gasped. 'But we need it right away.'

'It won't take long,' he replied and proceeded to explain that composing the twenty-odd minutes of music required would barely take him a week, and he was as good as his word. He attended only one run-through of the play, made careful notes and when the score was delivered, every fanfare and musical bridge was correctly timed to the very last second. A piano version was made to enable the witches to rehearse their 'Double double' bits and eventually the whole thing was recorded by HMV on acetate one-sided 78s with thirty minutes of the London Philharmonic Orchestra conducted by Ernest Irving. They over-ran the recording session by an incredible amount of overtime and poor John had to produce a personal cheque as nobody would leave the studio until every last penny had been paid. Came the day when there was a run-through of the play with the music, and in the empty theatre I felt like Ludwig of Bavaria listening to the final versions of *Tannhauser* or *Lohengrin*.

John had put together a tremendously complicated effects score with wind howling at all the climaxes, bells ringing, doors being hammered on, etc, and the only way all this could be co-ordinated was for two operators—Mary and Viola—to manipulate the pana-tropes—gramophones with pick-up arms that could be spotted on to any given groove of the 78s—with the effects on one machine and the Walton music on the other. John kept changing his mind and adding or subtracting effects with the result that finally there were one hundred and forty separate cues for effects, while the music was fed in to complement or underline the action. After the final matinee, John came up to Viola and asked her to add another wind cue to the plot.

'But, Mr Gielgud, there's only one more performance,' wailed the harassed stage manager.

'Yes, I know, but I *would* like to hear it just once,' said John, and who could resist him?

§

Sir John was called upon, at the midnight hour, to redirect a production of *The Heiress*, starring his old friend Sir Ralph Richardson. It did not take their saviour long to realize that drastic steps would be necessary to salvage the production.

Of the positioning of the cast for one scene, he remarked that they were 'strung out from side to side like a football team'.

§

Lord Olivier:
It was lovely to be with Glennie (Byam Shaw) again and with Johnnie Gielgud as our director; though, as twenty years before in *Romeo*, he did not always agree with what I was trying to do, we had enough mutual fondness and respect to recognize that perfect agreement in matters of characterization would never be ours, not in this world; and so peaceful co-operation was possible. He still had the disconcerting habit of changing moves at every single rehearsal; of course a director has the right to change his mind, but after almost four weeks and with the opening night looming closer, I began to be nervous that the occasion would be a shambles, with an utterly confused company knowing neither the timing nor the placing of the moves. Noel Coward once said that the only real use of a director was to stop the actors from bumping into each other; at

the rate our *Twelfth Night* was going our first performance would have been more like a game of Blind Man's Buff than anything else.

Sensing disaster, I had to talk to Glen and explain that none of us had yet been allowed to do the same things two days running. He asked John Gielgud to join us, and at the risk of hurting his feelings I asked him to leave the company at the point we had got to and let us go over and over it for a couple of days until we knew the moves well enough to do a run-through without a stop; then at least he himself would be able to see his own mistakes if there were any, and if he needed to make more changes he could make as many as he chose, since we would at least know what we were changing *from*. I'm afraid he was a bit hurt by the suggestion that he should quit his own rehearsals, but for the sake of avoiding a disaster I had to be firm and insist. At the end of the two days we were able to offer him a clean run-through. As I suspected, he did not find that he had to alter that much, and he recognized that I had respected his production and, as I had promised, made not a single change in it.

$$\hat{q}$$

Sir John may have that somewhat trying side to his nature, but he can also redeem the most exhausting rehearsal. Judi Dench: I met him and was in *The Cherry Orchard* with him in 1961, as Anya. And I had the most terrible time with Michel Saint-Denis, the director. A terrible time. He kept saying to me, 'You've got to prove to me that you deserve the job.' One day after we'd run it and I was a gibbering mess, John just said, 'If that had been for me that you had been acting that would have been just right.'

And I thought, then I shall change my sights. I

shall simply veer round as a kind of weathercock and I shall just perform for John. I shall perform for his next compliment. And that's what got me through it.

Sir John's Great Roles

Sir John:
I have a particular aversion to the hackneyed Gothic style of decoration for *Hamlet*, in which the King and Queen look like playing-cards, and Hamlet like an overgrown Peter Pan.

◊

Lord Olivier:
I remember when we worked together in that early production of *Romeo and Juliet*, how I was the whipping boy and John was the adored god. At that time John was the king of the West End, he was already a huge star and quite rightly enjoyed it. I don't say that with envy, for indeed I was a star as well, but I was still considered a movie actor. I was more of an upstart, I suppose—in the eyes of the Establishment, that is, not in my own eyes, certainly not in my own. I have always had that rod of steel in my make-up; flexible, but there. I have always very much believed in myself, as of course every actor must.

Dame Sybil Thorndike, on Gielgud's first *Hamlet*, at the Old Vic, 1929:

I never hoped to see *Hamlet* played as in one's dreams . . . tonight it was *Hamlet* Complete . . . I've had an evening of being swept right off my feet into another life—far more real than the life I live in, and moved, moved beyond words.

◊

Sir John Gielgud, describing his interpretation of *Richard II*, also at the Old Vic in the same season, 1929:

He was a shallow, spoiled young man, vain of his looks, with lovely things to say. I fancied myself no end in the part, but even that seemed to help my acting of it.

◊

A German version of *Hamlet*, with Alexander Moissi, played concurrently with Sir John's in the West End in 1929/30 in a neighbouring theatre. Gielgud recalled going to see his rival in a matinée before his own evening performance:

Moissi appeared to be permanently sorry for himself, crying into his handkerchief in the Nunnery scene, and finally stabbing the King in the back. I was introduced to him backstage and he looked me up and down and said, through his interpreter, 'Oh, you play it in the Spanish style, I see.' (My costume had a high white collar and black trunk hose.) That was all he said. He was wearing a costume that somehow combined Peter Pan with the Middle Ages and it did not suit him very well.

◊

The coexistence of two *Hamlets* placed a strain on London's supply of skulls! Sir John again, on the same West End production of 1929:

The very first night in the West End gave the stage management some alarming moments. The scene in the churchyard was played on a platform. Below this was the real stage, which served for the bottom of the grave. Here the skulls were carefully placed. It seemed to me, when I walked on with Horatio, that an air of thoughtfulness, one might have said of strain, hung over the First Grave Digger. I suddenly saw what had happened a few lines before we came to the best part of the scene. The skull was missing. And soon I must begin the 'Alas, poor Yorick' speech, holding it in my hands. Should I orate over an imaginary skull? I dared not hope that the audience's imagination would follow me so far. I suddenly decided to cut thirty lines. I jumped to 'But soft, but soft awhile—here comes the King', the words which introduce Ophelia's funeral procession which was fortunately forming in the wings at that very moment. There was a short pause while the surprised mourners hurried to their places, then the procession entered. I learned afterwards that owing to the rake of the stage the skulls had rolled out of the grave-digger's reach. There was nothing to be done, though the distracted stage manager had tried, without avail, to borrow another skull from the Globe Theatre next door, where Alexander Moissi was playing *Hamlet* in a German version.

◊

Sir John Gielgud:

When it came to casting the boy (in *The Lady's Not For Burning*) Binkie Beaumont had no doubts: 'We must have Richard Burton, of course.' I said. 'Who's he? . . . He turned up at rehearsal the next day and I realized that he was perfect for the part. I never had to tell him anything at all, except not to yawn so much when he wanted his lunch.

§

James Agate, on Gielgud's 1944 *Hamlet*:

Mr Gielgud is now completely and authoritatively master of this tremendous part. He is, we feel, this generation's rightful tenant of this 'monstrous Gothic castle of a poem'. He has acquired an almost Irvingesque quality of pathos, and in the passages after the play scene an incisiveness, a raillery, a mordancy worthy of the Old Man. He imposes on us this play's questing feverishness. The middle act gives us ninety minutes of high excitement and assured virtuosity; Forbes-Robertson was not more bedazzling in the 'O, what a rogue and peasant slave' soliloquy. In short, I hold that this is, and is likely to remain, the best Hamlet of our time.

§

Having made Gordon Daviot's *Richard of Bordeaux* his own, Sir John was succeeded in the title-role by Glen Byam Shaw. He went to see the new star of the play with Richard Clowes.

Richard Clowes to John Gielgud: 'John dear, I know the play moved you, but I did once see you lean forward and count the house through your tears.'

'Dickie Clowes, that's a wicked thing to say. Actually it wasn't at all bad, I was surprised . . .'

§

Lord Olivier:

I thought his first *Hamlet* was wonderful, because he didn't allow himself to do that, he didn't sing. But as time went by I believe he sang it more and more. His fifth or sixth performance of *Hamlet*, as far as I was concerned, was a complete aria. For me this was a great disappointment. I said to myself, 'That's wonderful in its way, but has he not gone backwards?'

◊

Sir John Gielgud:
Edith Evans grew to hate her success as Lady Bracknell, though it was perhaps the most popular and famous of all her great impersonations. She was staying at my cottage in Essex one weekend just before the War when I suggested a possible revival of the Wilde play. I took a copy from the bookshelf and we read the handbag scene together to the other guests. After the laughter had died down Edith handed me back the book and remarked gravely, 'I know those sort of women. They ring the bell and tell you to put a lump of coal on the fire!'

◊

Bernard Levin:
The first productions I ever saw were also among the best I have ever seen, those magical performances in the Old Vic's days of glory in St Martin's Lane, and John Gielgud's last *Hamlet*, at the Haymarket Theatre in 1944, at the end of which I walked all the way home, a distance of some four miles, without being in any way conscious of my surroundings until I found myself, to my extreme astonishment, putting my key in the door.

◊

Donald Sinden, describing Gielgud's ENSA *Hamlet* of 1945:

The untold depths of misery he could dredge up in any of Hamlet's lines, the gravity he gave to 'A little more than kin, and less than kind.' After Hamlet had seen and talked with his father's ghost he says to himself:

> The time is out of joint: O cursed spite,
> That ever I was born to set it right!

then he turns to Horatio and Marcellus and says, 'Nay, come, let's go together'. I wish I could describe how many facets Gielgud gave to that simple line.

I learned from that one line what infinite possibilities are open to an actor.

♦

Richard Pasco:

This story is probably apocryphal. It supposedly took place during a Stratford season in the early Fifties. Sir John had had an exhausting week playing eight performances of *King Lear* with Dame Peggy Ashcroft playing Cordelia. On the Saturday night, after a gruelling matinée and evening performance, on picking up the 'dead' Cordelia in the wings prior to the devastatingly tragic entrance of 'Howl, howl, howl etc.,' he was apparently overheard to say, as he lifted up Cordelia, 'Oh God, I wish I'd never taken up the bloody classics!'

♦

Sir John recalls advice given him by Harley Granville-Barker for his 1940 *King Lear*:

He was quite impersonal, calling everybody by the name of their part or by their own surnames—none of the 'dears' and 'darlings' in which we are apt to indulge in the theatre . . . one day (after an early reading) he said to me, 'Well, you've got two lines right. Of course, you are an ash and this part demands an oak, but we'll see what can be done.'

♀

Sir John Gielgud:
I know *Romeo and Juliet* by heart, and I have played Romeo three times, yet I cannot say that I ever pleased myself in it . . . and in this early Romeo (of 1922) I looked a sight. I was given white tights with soles attached to them underneath and no shoes. My feet looked enormous, and it was most uncomfortable to fight or run about. My wig was coal-black, and parted in the middle. Wearing an orange make-up and a very low-necked doublet, I look, in the photographs, a mixture of Rameses of Egypt and a Victorian matron.

♀

That particular production was clearly not an absolute triumph. Sir John again:
A wealthy lady who lived a little way out of London invited us to play the balcony scene on her lawn one Sunday night . . . I ran across a flower-bed to my place below the window from which Gwen (Ffrangcon-Davies) was leaning (her wig looking strangely orange in the moonlight), and found that I had to risk life and limb on a very rickety espalier before I could touch her hand with mine. I looked round desperately to invoke the moon, but realized at last that it was shining on the wrong side of the house. Our lines were punctuated by our hostess's murmuring in a rich Dutch accent, 'Oh! it's so r-r-romantic!' and the wrigglings and slappings of the other guests who were vainly battling with mosquitoes.

♀

46

Sir John, on the problems of rehearsing Romeo, here in 1924:

At the dress-rehearsal we (Gwen Ffrangcon-Davies played Juliet) were both so full of pins that we could hardly embrace . . . Romeo is a very long and arduous part and I was no good at the sword-fights. Scott Sunderland was playing Mercutio in a very violent style. He used to knock me about on the stage which made me nervous and threw me off balance.

◊

Although Alan Bennett's play *Forty Years On* eventually became a great success, earning golden opinions for all, including Sir John, who played the headmaster, its pre-West End run was dogged by problems and misunderstandings.

Alan Bennett: Tonight my parents come. They have obviously been a bit mystified by the play, and sit in my dressing-room in awkward silence as my dresser, a veteran of the music halls, puts away my stuff. After he's gone, it transpires they thought *he* was Sir John Gielgud and was ignoring them deliberately because he was unhappy with the play.

◊

Sir John Gielgud:

The last time I ever played *Hamlet* was in the Cairo Opera House. It was a school matinée, packed with children, and as we started the play I thought, 'Well, this is the last time I shall ever play this wonderful part. I'm forty-five and it's quite time to give it up.' Early on in the performance the unfortunate man who played Horatio fell into my arms in an epileptic fit on the line, 'My Lord, I think I saw him yesternight.' The audience was bewildered as I shouted to the prompt corner, rather crossly, 'Drop the curtain. Put something between his teeth. Fetch the understudy.' The understudy came, rescued from the bowels of the theatre where he was making up for Guildenstern, and did not know a line. When he pointed to the Ghost and said, 'Look, my Lord, it comes,' I said, 'No, you fool, the other way!' or words to that effect. Fortunately, the epileptic Horatio recovered the next day, but I could never quite forgive him for ruining my final performance of *Hamlet*.

ò

Sir John:

A week before we were due to open (in *Hamlet* in 1936) in Toronto I was wounded in the arm rehearsing the fight. I fence abominably. In London I had nearly cut Benvolio's eye out at rehearsal, and in *Romeo* I so badly wounded the actor who played Tybalt that he had to leave the cast for a week. In New York our instructor rashly allowed us to rehearse with real Elizabethan swords sharpened on both edges. This time I was the injured party. I was removed to a neighbouring surgery where I was given gas while several stitches were put in my arm.

ò

Sir John recalls a *Hamlet* he took to India and the Far East under the aegis of ENSA:

I besought the actress who was playing Gertrude not to fling her heavy train to one side in the final scene, as clouds of dust flew up to choke me as I lay on the floor in the throes of approaching death. 'Oh, dear,' she said, 'I don't really feel like a Queen unless I can fling my train.'

ò

Sir John on another *Hamlet*, this time in 1934:

One night, during one of the intervals in *Hamlet*, Frank Vosper was visited by an Army major who told him how much he was enjoying the performance. He was not the type of playgoer one would have expected to relish Shakespearean tragedy and we were all delighted to hear that he was enjoying himself. Then came the moment in the final scene when Claudius says, 'Cousin Hamlet, you know the wager.' None of us knew where to look when Frank, still thinking of his visitor and quite unaware of his mistake, demanded sonorously, 'Cousin Hamlet, you know the major!'

The Relationship of the Three Knights

Sir Peter Hall:
First day of *The Tempest*, my first National Theatre production . . . Larry (Olivier) was in earnest attendance. This upset John Gielgud, though he masked it, perfectly mannered Edwardian that he is. Larry had asked if he could come to the first rehearsal and really I felt in no position to say no. He busied himself by wandering round shaking hands with everybody.

Took John Gielgud off to my office for lunch and we had only been seated for two minutes when Larry reappeared. He sat and chatted, making Gielgud feel uneasy. It is extraordinary to watch these two giants. Gielgud obviously is disturbed by Larry, and Larry knows it.

◊

Lord Olivier:
John is a very sweet man, but he seems to say rather

more critical things about me than he does about Ralph. He probably wouldn't agree with this, and I've more than likely got it all wrong; I mean I'm sure he's fond of me really, but somehow something still niggles in the back of my mind. He harks back every now and again to how terrible he thought I was as Romeo; but that was over forty-five years ago. Surely you don't have to harbour unpleasant thoughts about people for forty-five years? I know that my Romeo, to say the least, was controversial, but it was also ultimately a success. At the time, of course, opinion was very much out of my favour. I was a slightly bigger success than John as Mercutio, but he made a vastly bigger success than I did as Romeo, and that hurt because Romeo was what I saw myself as . . .

◊

Harold Hobson:
Shortly after John Gielgud was knighted, Olivier began to be concerned that John Gielgud was not being given the recognition for his work that was his due. The *Evening Standard*, as it then was, inaugurated a series of annual awards, which gained great prestige, and one day I received a message that Olivier wanted to see me. A superb Rolls arrived at my home, and carried me in splendour to the great man. Olivier was much agitated. He had the year before received the coveted *Standard* award for Best Actor, and he had heard that it was likely that he would get it the second time. 'This is distressing,' he said. 'Getting an award means nothing to me. It makes no difference at all to my reputation. But if I get it again, it will be another slap in the face for Johnnie (Gielgud). It is a cruelty that mustn't be allowed to happen. I want you to resign from the selection committee.' I admired his sympathy for Gielgud and I admire it now. But what that had to do with my resigning from

the committee (of which I was not an important or influential member) I have never been able to understand. But I saw that Olivier meant well, and so I resigned. The award was duly offered to Olivier, and, somewhat to my surprise, he accepted it.

◊

Sir John Gielgud:
Larry (Olivier) lives *en prince*.

◊

Sir Peter Hall:
John Gielgud phoned . . . He said Larry (Olivier) came round after the performance of *No Man's Land* on Friday and told him and Ralph that he couldn't hear either of them, and went to sleep. He threatened to return on Monday night—the play's last performance—when he hoped he'd be able to hear it. Ralph is very upset: why is Larry so harsh? John, who is furious, is more down to earth; he says he suspects Larry is going deaf.

◊

Lord Olivier:
Watching John (Gielgud) and Ralph (Richardson) spark off each other over the past few years on stage and on screen has been a real joy: the contrasts rich in flavour, like eating a good meal, looking at a fine painting, or listening to Mozart. They were so in tune, though able to descant to each other at will, like a brilliant double act. That wicked glance from Ralph at the audience saying, 'This is my turn, look at me,' and then John gently steering the eyes in his direction, with complete authority.

They were in such charge of their acting machinery, would that they could have gone on forever, but now sadly the elder of the party has gone and the two-man band has been reduced to a single turn again.

It was a dream to watch them, all guns blazing, and we must be grateful to the inspired managements who had the insight to put them together.

◊

Sir John Gielgud:

It is wonderful to play with somebody who is so absolutely opposed to you in temperament: we (Sir John and Sir Ralph) are a tremendous contrast in personality. Now, after so many performances and interviews together, we say we are becoming like the broker's men in *Cinderella*. People even mix us up and greet us by each other's names, particularly in America where titles often confuse the public.

◊

Sir Alec Guinness:

A few years ago, after Ralph and Mu (Lady Richardson) had given me dinner at a smart London hotel, we walked slowly across the road to his car while he fumbled in a pocket for a pound note. An obsequious commissionaire, with a sharp eye for a good tip, followed us, raising his top-hat and saying, 'Good night, Sir Alec. Nice to see you, sir. And good night to you, too, Sir John.' 'Bastard!' Ralph muttered, putting away the money. However, as we reached the car I noticed him surreptitiously take out the note again and slip it to the man.

◊

Sir Peter Hall:
A great event. I took Ralph Richardson and John Gielgud for a tour of the South Bank. It was very funny. John, who is nearly seventy, treated Ralph, who is seventy-one, as if he were an extremely aged and endearing relative up from the country, unused to city ways: 'Mind those holes . . .' 'Don't trip over those wires.' They were both in long coats and large trilbys, Ralph sporting a stick. They could have been nothing but actors. And great ones too. Both sleek with success.

◊

Sir Ralph Richardson on Sir John Gielgud:
I can never get him to lose his temper.

◊

Sir Alec Guinness:
A day or two after an abortive dinner at the Connaught, Sir Alec was telephoned by Sir Ralph:
'Did you walk all the way home?' I asked.
'Yes,' he replied. 'But I sat for a while on a bench in Oxford Street. It was very nice until a chap on a bicycle stopped by me. 'I know you,' he said. 'You're Sir John Gielgud,' he said. 'Fuck off!' I said. Then I walked home. It was a lovely night for walking. So many stars.'

◊

From a Michael Parkinson interview:
Parkinson: What's the difference between your acting and Gielgud's?
Sir Ralph: I'd say he's a much better actor than I am. I admire him so much, his range is enormous. *Richard II*, *Richard III* . . . he's a great speaker, the finest speaker of verse in the world today.

Parkinson: Aren't there parts that he can't play that you could?

Sir Ralph: Well I wouldn't like to talk about that. So . . . let's talk about motor bikes!

(Sir John never appeared as *Richard III*.)

◊

Sir Ralph Richardson:

Sir Ralph's first impressions of Sir John were not favourable; his acting used to 'keep him out of the theatre'. 'I found his clothes extravagant, I found his conversation flippant. He was the New Young Man of his time and I didn't like him . . . I was always rather amazed at him—a kind of brilliant sort of butterfly, while I was a gloomy sort of boy.'

◊

Sir John Gielgud:

He (Sir Ralph Richardson) is inclined to despise the petty accessories of theatrical life which appeal so strongly to me—the gossip, the theatrical columns in the newspapers, the billing and the photographs in the front of the house—and it is probably only by chance that he has found a creative outlet on the stage. He might have succeeded equally well as a mechanic, a doctor, or an airman. Unlike me he is intensely interested in machinery and in all the intricate details of science and engineering.

◊

Sir John Gielgud:

Sometimes (during the 1930 *King Lear* at Old Vic) the audience could not resist such majesty, especially in a farewell production, and at least three nights a week I came on to applause. This uncertainty started a little joke between Ralph Richardson and myself. He was on the stage before me, and as I prepared to enter, encumbered by my own magnificence, he would look slyly in my direction as I stood in the wings, hiding his smile behind his thick, mask-like make-up. (Ralph always designed elaborate make-ups, made careful drawings for them beforehand, and carried them out in great detail with shadows and highlights, scoffing at our comparatively slapdash efforts at disguise. He achieved striking results, but his method stylized his appearance and made him apt to look different from anyone else on the stage.) In the meantime I was trying to amass my eighty years and my large effects of majesty in the wings. If I failed to get the round of applause as I mounted my throne the expression of amused triumph on Ralph's face would be almost too much for me. It was fortunate that I had to turn away from the audience for a moment before I faced them and began, 'Attend the lords of France and Burgundy . . .'

◊

Sir Ralph Richardson:
On Sir John's manner of self-expression. He didn't employ the 'precision of the range rifle' but went off more 'like a catherine wheel'.

◊

Derek Granger:
If Olivier is the king, the lion, the god, the hero and sometimes the black villain of the trio (Oedipus, Henry V, Richard III); if Richardson is the transmuted stuff of ordinary play with a pipeline to the dreams and longings of the common man (Peer Gynt, Falstaff, Cyrano and the 'little man' heroes of Priestley and Sheriff); then

John (Gielgud) is supremely the prince, the poet and philosopher, the aesthete and the dandy (Richard II, Prospero, Valentine, Benedick, Jack Worthing). If Olivier is fire, thunder, animal magnetism and danger; if Richardson is bemused wonder, slyness, and compassion; then John is poetic sensibility, philosophical introspection, detachment, reason, quicksilver wit and everything that is expressive of an intense inner life.

φ

Charles Sturridge:
There was never any kind of doubt about wanting to have John Gielgud play Charles Ryder's father (in *Brideshead Revisited*). One might have thought about Ralph Richardson, had he been alive, but Gielgud was the obvious choice as someone able to conduct that particularly vicious kind of war with his son. The question was, would we be able to get him? Less a question of choosing him than persuading him to do it. Olivier was furious—he had only read part when we started to shoot and finished it while we were filming. He read the book and was very upset that he wasn't playing the part of Mr Ryder because he thought it was the best, the funniest part. And anyway, I think he was only doing it to be naughty. And he loved the idea of Lord Marchmain's death scene. But then, given the chance, he would have played all the parts. He just loves playing comedy.

φ

Lord Olivier:
Ralph Richardson, John Gielgud and I competed with each other in those scenes when we were all together in Tony Palmer's marathon *Wagner*—there was very little else to do. So often the case when you're

blockbustering. We certainly competed in the classical stage roles.

◊

Sir Peter Hall:
Finally you have to compare the three great actors of that generation—Olivier, Richardson and Gielgud. I have worked with them all and knew them well. Larry seemed to me to be always redefining things in brilliant technical terms—making his art more and more extraordinary and sharp: a dazzling technical display. Ralph Richardson was like a wonderful craftsman, painstakingly carving a piece of wood each night at the theatre and making new discoveries. Out of his craft he made art. Gielgud was an improviser—like a wonderful butterfly he sped all over the place, creating new shapes, new forms and living dangerously. Their rhythms and their attitudes were totally different. So I suppose finally Olivier was the heroic actor, the man who could display with genius. Gielgud was the romantic actor. And Richardson was the actor who told us about the poetry of the people.

◊

Lord Olivier:
Do you know the most affecting thing about my 'affair' with *Richard III*? John Gielgud passed on to me the sword Edmund Kean had used in his performance. A great and unselfish and typical act of friendship, but a greater act of love for the art of acting. Actors' camaraderie stretches back to Shakespeare, at least, and it must continue.

◊

Judi Dench:
He's revered, isn't he, Larry? But he's less approachable, perhaps, than John. Ralph Richardson was worshipped, because of his eccentricity. John for his vulnerability, perhaps. When one says, 'common touch', John is the last person you could say that about. And *yet* . . . it's something to do with his shyness and his brick-dropping and his elegance. He is infinitely approachable.

◊

Lord Olivier:
We were, and indeed are, very different actors and people. I will always be an active actor, and John is a passive one. I'm a peripheral player who goes out to the character, whereas he stays in the centre, finds something in the part that will suit him, then pulls it in towards himself. I went for the physical, the heroics if you like, whereas John was always the poet, the ephemerist, head upturned towards the stars. I always appeared to be firmly astride this earth, eyes level on the horizon. Two very different actors, both with one thing in mind: success.

◊

Donald Sinden:
I have abject admiration for John Gielgud: he is everything I could not be. If Olivier is a physical actor, Gielgud is cerebral.

◊

Lord Olivier:
John has a dignity, a majesty which suggests that he was born with a crown on his head; on the other hand

my persona is that of a man who has plucked the crown up and placed it on himself. I am Bosworth Field and Agincourt; and John is Pomfret Castle.

◊

Emlyn Williams recalls an evening when he, his wife Molly, Angela Baddeley and her husband Glen Byam Shaw encountered a distressed Laurence Olivier:

We tried to cheer him up, to no avail. 'I'm washed up, I'll never make it . . .' It was incredible. Then he reminded us that during the last couple of years, he had been slipping. 'Hollywood just didn't want to know, Garbo turned me down for *Queen Christina*, *Ringmaster* was a flop . . .' A month before, within a few days of Vivien Leigh's triumph, he had gone into management with a play called *Golden Arrow*, starring himself and introducing a new young actress, a gorgeous redhead who had stolen the play from under him: Greer Garson. 'I had a dull part, but people said I was dull in it—and now there's talk of me alternating Romeo and Mercutio with Johnnie G., imagine me speaking verse next to that one, I'll sink without trace . . .'

Sir John's Recent Work

Sir John Gielgud:
When I was young, we wore our best suits to rehearsal and called the leading man 'sir'—now they wear jeans and call me John.

Lord Olivier:
Looking back, I suppose we all took ourselves rather seriously: when we let the humour and vulnerability creep in, we get much closer to the truth. This was especially true of John Gielgud in his early days. Now that he appears to regard himself with a sense of humour he has become a much finer actor. Once he threw off the finery and took an honest look at himself in the glass, his acting became much richer and more truthful. His performances in *Home* and *No Man's Land*, for instance, showed him at his stunning best. He is a character actor and it is good to see he's got holes in his socks. He has a delicious sense of humour and at least he is letting it grin through.

Gary O'Connor:

In rehearsal Gielgud expressed his nervousness about *Home* in a variety of ways; he developed the weird habit of taking from his pocket a pair of scissors and cutting out those sections of the text which did not concern him or his part until his copy was in ribbons. (When the play became a great success, it was a showcase for the new informal style of Ralph Richardson's and John Gielgud's acting. Thus, John Gielgud was reported as saying later to the Los Angeles Times: 'Now I try not to speak too perfectly.')

◊

Lindsay Anderson:

I remember a late rehearsal of *Home*, a run-through at the Royal Court just before we went down to Brighton for our one week out of town. It had been a beautiful performance—with the actors wearing their costumes, or part of them, for the first time. At the end there were tears in my eyes. I came down from the Circle where I had been watching the run-through into the Stalls. John was there, changing into his own trousers. 'That was beautiful,' I said, 'I was really moved at the end.' John looked up, pausing as he inserted his leg into his trousers. 'Don't you think it's a bit short?' he said, in those famous clipped tones. I could only laugh as his impeccable professionalism cut through my (to him) irrelevant emotion. John's artistry is grounded always in a craftsmanship that admits of no indulgence. I wish we had been able to work together again. But *Home* remains the experience of a lifetime.

◊

David Storey, writer of *Home*:

The beginning of rehearsals for *Home* was like watching two horses (Sir John and Sir Ralph) galloping along while, perched on a delicately-fashioned carriage behind, a driver called out, "Whoa! Stop!" finally turning to his fellow passenger and saying, wryly, 'Well, we'd better let them have a run . . .' If *The Contractor* (Storey's previous play) had seen the empirical method of directing at its most demanding, *Home* saw it at its most discreet:

'It isn't possible for an actor to sit on a stage without moving, Lindsay, for twenty-five minutes.'

'Is it twenty-five minutes?'

'It feels like twenty-five.'

'Move, in that case, if you feel like it, John.'

Until a point had been reached:

'It's strange, but once sitting here, I don't feel I want to move again.'

'Don't, in that case.'

◊

The closeness of the acting partnership which formed between Sir John and Sir Ralph allowed for spontaneous performances for the benefit of waiting journalists:

Sir Ralph: Shall we live it up now?

Sir John: Certainly.

Sir Ralph: You're looking very well by the way.

Sir John: Thank you.

Sir Ralph: I haven't seen much of you lately.

Sir John: We meet in costume.

Sir Ralph: We meet as other people.

◊

Judi Dench:

You remember with Ralph Richardson in *No Man's Land* when he came on with the glasses and the sandals.

And Ralph said, 'I know what we'll do. You're good at crying and I'm good at falling down and that's how we'll play the part.'

ȹ

Lord Olivier:
The pain behind the glasses in *No Man's Land* was electrifying . . . the bare soul covered with a thin veneer of sophistication. You could see the clouds passing across his face like a day in an English acre. The sun popping out on the odd moment giving a façade of warmth and happiness . . . not a summer sun, a winter sun. That performance created a reality that I've always fought for.

ȹ

Sir Peter Hall:
At rehearsal (for *No Man's Land*) this afternoon John (Gielgud) asked Harold (Pinter) what the Briggs/Spooner scene was for at the beginning of Act II. What did it give the audience? What did it convey? Harold paused. 'I'm afraid I cannot answer questions like that, John. My work is just what it is. I am sorry.'

ȹ

Michael Feast:
I played the non-speaking Christ-figure whom Sir John as the Grand Inquisitor interrogates and finally sends to his death, in *The Grand Inquisitor* (from *The Brothers Karamazov*) for the BBC Open University. It was done while we were playing *No Man's Land* and Sir John with characteristic kindness asked for me to play the part as he said he didn't want to spend an hour looking into a stranger's face while he spoke the lines.

Sir John Mills:

Veterans was, I thought, a hilarious comedy, but full of 'in' jokes and some scenes which contained language that was definitely not for the ears of Auntie Mabel or the grandchildren. Edinburgh received the play in shocked, stony silence. John and I got letters informing us that we should be ashamed of appearing in a play that contained such disgusting language. One letter to me enclosed a ten-shilling note. The sender wrote, 'I enclose this more in sorrow than in anger, to my hero Scott of the Antarctic, who must be very hard up.' Nottingham reacted in more or less the same way. It was the time of the power cuts, and I remember being almost grateful at times when we were blacked out in the middle of the play. 'Hang on,' the management said. 'It's Brighton next week. They're much more sophisticated. Things will be very different there.'

Truer words have never been spoken—things *were* different. Half-way through the first act a riot broke out in the theatre. There were shouts of 'Disgusting!' 'How dare you?' etc. from all over the house. Johnny G. was on stage at the time, and I was waiting in the wings. His face was a study; he couldn't believe it was happening. I had received 'the bird' before, in cabaret, but for one of our leading classical actor-knights it was a first experience, and a hair-raising one.

Mary (Lady Mills), who happened to be standing at the back row of the dress circle watching this incredible audience reaction, saw a very large man get up out of his seat, and in a voice loud enough to drown the rest of the hubbub, address his fellow customers in the circle: 'I have been coming to this theatre for years, and this is the last time. John Gielgud and John Mills should be ashamed of themselves. There are ladies in this audience, and I've never heard such disgusting, filthy language in all my life; and if you're not leaving, I am.' He then pushed his way through to the end of the row. As he passed Mary on the top of the stairs, purple with rage, she heard him mutter, 'And I paid good money to see them two fuckers.'

◊

Michael Feast:

My time with Sir John on *No Man's Land* was very enjoyable and I felt on less of a pupil-teacher footing . . . One of my abiding memories and one that still makes me smile to recall it is of hearing Sir John and Sir Ralph greet each other on stage each night before the curtain went up. I would hear over the tannoy in my dressing-room the two pairs of footsteps and then 'Hullo Johnny,' 'Hullo Ralphie,' and they would chatter on about their various days until just before the curtain rose . . . My other more general memory of that job was of the two Sirs' obvious love for each other. In particular, I felt that Sir John took great delight in Sir Ralph's eccentric naughtiness. I still remember vividly Sir Ralph asking Pinter one day, 'I see I have a silence marked here in the text and then a pause. Tell me, dear fellow, how many pauses make a silence, would you say?'

Pinter looked impassive and serious, as only Pinter can. I'm sure he was mentally debating how much he was being sent up or how serious Sir Ralph was being. At last Pinter said flatly, 'Oh, I should say five pauses to a silence, Ralph.' 'I see,' said Sir Ralph. 'Thank you very much indeed.' All through this, as through many other of Sir Ralph's marvellously quotable verbal expeditions, Sir John's face was a picture, glowing with enjoyment and pride in his old friend's mischievousness, sometimes spilling over into boyish and irresistible peals and chuckles at something particularly hilarious. I think they were very great comrades.

Charles Sturridge:
There's an effect that a great actor has on the set which is electrifying and which John Gielgud certainly has. It somehow forces all the other actors to concentrate and makes every member of the crew try hard to be at his best.

◊

Lindsay Anderson:
We played together in Hugh Hudson's film *Chariots of Fire* and it was there that I learned just what it means (particularly to fellow actors) to be a Star. Not that, in John's case at least, this implies any conscious decision or way of behaving. Nobody could be less pretentious or less assuming. But the wholeness and intensity of concentration on the character he was playing challenged one, taking part in the same scene, to play with that same intensity and concentration.

◊

Michael Feast:
We had a tremendously gruelling technical rehearsal for *The Tempest* which had gone on all day and far into the night. We were all exhausted and wandering around backstage at the Vic like zombies. I recall sitting with a glass of wine in Dennis Quilley's dressing-room chatting with Dennis and Arthur Lowe and they both said that they had never known a technical like it. Around ten or eleven o'clock, Sir John fell through the trap door downstage right which was about to reveal Ferdinand and Miranda playing chess. I don't remember if he walked into it or if it had opened accidentally. It doesn't matter—the effect on everybody was electrifying. Was Sir John hurt? People ran from everywhere. The two actors waiting beneath (Rupert Fraser

and Jenny Agutter) were shocked and shaken. Sir John was shocked, bruised, but basically unhurt. He was incredibly good-humoured about it and, although at this time he must have been terribly tired, insisted on pressing on. In fact, rehearsals were terminated not long after this incident as I think the entire company was in shock.

◊

Sir Peter Hall:
Went this afternoon to see *Providence*. Gielgud is superb. I rang John and told him how wonderful I thought his performance. He said he was delighted because it was his first butch part!

◊

Charles Sturridge:
I was lucky enough to get him (for *Brideshead Revisited*) at a period of his life when he began to enjoy film-making. I think he'd always been rather irritated by it as something he didn't fully understand or much enjoy. One got the feeling that he didn't think there were many performances on film that he considered important to his career. He has now, I think, begun to understand and relish film as a way of creating a performance. The mark of a great film actor is that when you see a performance on film as opposed to in front of you, you suddenly see many more things than you'd actually seen when it was being shot. And I think that's certainly true of Gielgud's performance as Ryder's father, which I think gets funnier the more you see it.

◊

Sir Peter Hall:
Delightful lunch at the Garrick Club with Gielgud . . .
John was very spry. He's delighted about his success in
the Alain Resnais film *Providence* and said with giggles
of pleasure that he did feel a little embarrassed having
such good notices for a movie at the same time as Larry
was getting such odd notices for his Harold Robbins
picture, *The Betsy*.

◊

Jeremy Irons:
Though deeply polite and charming, Sir John never-
theless always remained a little remote (during the filming of *Brideshead*) and while the scene was being set up
could always be found snuggled up in some quiet corner, just within earshot, doing *The Times* crossword.

◊

Charles Sturridge:
We did a first take of the scene where Charles Ryder
tells Ryder that he's going to be divorced from his first
wife in order to be able to marry Julia. It's late in the
story, and John and Jeremy (Irons) were the oldest one
sees them in the film. They both had lots of ageing
make-up on and were drinking tea. After the first take,
I went over to Gielgud and started to talk in a rather
rapid-fire way about some of the ideas I had about how
the scene should go. I was really rather nervous. He
looked me up and down after my frantic five-minute
speech, and after a pause said, 'Oh, so you want me to
be funnier? I think I can manage that.' Which is exactly
what I'd meant but hadn't dared say.

◊

Dirk Bogarde:

John's arrival (on the set of *Providence*) caused a different form of reverence. One which was well justified, although it fussed him greatly.

'I do wish they wouldn't keep *on* calling me *Sirjohn*,' he said one day. 'It's so frightfully inhibiting. Couldn't you ask them and Alain (Resnais) as well, just to call me "John" as everyone else does on a film? It saves time, you see. Of course I have asked them not to but they still do. I know Alain thinks that it is disrespectful, but *do* please ask them.'

I promised that I would try. 'It'll be difficult. After all, you must realize that you are one of the greatest living actors in the English-speaking world, you are knighted, you have had a tremendous career . . . they *will* find it disrespectful. The French hold their great performers in high esteem.'

'Well, it's very nice of them: but be a dear, and do what you can.'

'It'll be almost impossible. But if you find it irritating . . .'

'Well, you see,' he said, 'I've always been lucky in having very unsycophantic friends around me, who just say, 'Oh! Stick a crown on his head and shove him on.' It's *so* much more relaxing.'

In time he got his way: his very modesty, his generosity and warmth, made it possible; although I know that behind his back the troupe only ever referred to him as 'Sirjohn'. And that was that.

◊

Sir John Gielgud:

They offered me the part of the Emperor Tiberius (in *Caligula*) and I turned it down saying, 'This is pure pornography.' Gore Vidal, who wrote the original script, then wrote me a terrifically rude letter, saying how impertinent it was of me to refuse it and that if I knew what Tennessee Williams and Edward Albee said about me, I wouldn't be so grand. Terrible vituperation. Then they offered me another part that wasn't dirty and I rather shamefacedly took it. I played a whole scene in a bath of tepid water. It took three days to shoot and every two hours some horrible hags dragged me out, rubbed me down and put me back into the water again. Most extraordinary proceedings.

ℓ

Gore Vidal responded rather tersely when I asked him for a comment on the making and history of *Caligula*, enclosing Sir John's account of his involvement:

You do have it all wrong. When *Caligula* was my film, Claire Bloom wanted to play Drusilla. Unknown to me, the part of Tiberius was offered to John Gielgud who, to my relief, turned it down. Even then, his screen-acting was too obviously meretricious. We got Peter O'Toole. JG then, gratuitously, told Bloom she ought not to do the film, and I wrote him a disciplinary letter, telling him to mind his own business, and reminding him, unkindly, with what contempt Tenn Williams and Edward Albee regarded his critical acumen. As it turned out, Claire did not do the film but JG, of course, did—a small part. As I have never seen the film I cannot tell you just how bad it—and he—was.

ℓ

Charles Sturridge:
Gielgud is enormously open to suggest... He does a lot of preparatory work. He's hugely ...lligent. He knew a lot about Evelyn Waugh's fath...d how much *Brideshead* was based on Waugh's r...nship with his father. And he had a far clearer ...than I did, for

71

instance, about how to pronounce 'Orme-Herrick' because we were dealing with Edwardian accents and he is very accurate on that. He had been at Oxford in the 1920s, which is when Waugh was there. We also worked out that when working at the Playhouse in the Twenties he had broken into some rooms in University College. We established to a ninety-nine per cent certainty that these must have been the rooms which I occupied years later as an undergraduate. He was one of the few people on the set who remembered Oxford in the Twenties, the period we were involved with. And so he could speak with authority on pronunciation and in the endless debates about decor and manners and so on. In that area, as a source of research, he was the most accurate sort of person we could have had on the set.

The Voice

A leader from *The Times*, October 16th, 1987:

For half a century, four English players set standards for acting, speaking and professionalism that made the theatre for this country one of the artistic glories of the world. A little later than Sybil Thorndike's generation, a little earlier than Alec Guinness's, Laurence Olivier, Ralph Richardson, Peggy Ashcroft, and John Gielgud, made up a quartet of theatrical genius that has never been surpassed. Each brought a special quality into the theatre; Olivier had his blazing trumpet notes, Richardson his infinite cunning, Ashcroft her almost incredible versatility; and Gielgud the most beautiful, and most effectively used, theatrical voice this century has known . . .

Yet it is that voice, and what he has done with it, that defines him. It is exquisite, in the original senses—meaning of great beauty and keenly felt; it is thrilling; its delicate but ever-present vibrato keeps it warm and full of feeling; and a sharp, penetrating, wise and well-read intelligence (which Sir John is in the habit of gently and implausibly denying) fixes it, and what is said in it, for ever in the memory. Theatre-goers who have followed the careers of those four great players will remember always their performances; but in Gielgud's case, they also remember, in remarkable profusion, single lines, even phrases.

Once heard, never forgotten. From his Clarence in the Olivier film of *Richard III*: 'What scourge for perjury?' From his Benedick in *Much Ado About Nothing*: 'I do love nothing in the world so well as you.' From *The Winter's Tale*: 'Too hot, too hot.' And from the last of his four *Hamlets*, in 1944: 'Angels and ministers of grace defend us!'

◊

Sir Ralph Richardson:
Sir John Gielgud is 'a great conductor of his own music'.

◊

Sir John:
I received a good deal of personal criticism from a few discriminating friends, who told me that my mannerisms were becoming extremely pronounced, my walk as bad as ever, and my diction slovenly and affected. In one scene I had to quote Hamlet's 'Words, words, words.' My critics were perfectly right when they said I pronounced the line to sound like 'Wirds, wirds, wirds.'

◊

John Mortimer:
Some things become part of your whole life—and one of the best parts of mine is the voice of John Gielgud.

Dirk Bogarde's recollection of the filming of *Providence*:

Towards the end of work at the chateau, on June 3rd to be exact, Resnais (Alain, the director) had a birthday. The troupe decided to club together and get him a tape-recorder because he didn't own one, so we all put our offerings in a hat and someone went off to Lovely Limoges (as it had now become to us all) and bought the best model available . . . There was one small problem. They felt that it was essential that the first voice to be recorded on the virgin tape should be John's. And that he should say, 'This is John Gielgud wishing you a happy birthday, Alain, on behalf of the troupe and actors of *Providence*.' Or words to that effect. We all knew that Resnais was passionate about John's voice, indeed he had told me long before that he was determined to immortalize the splendour of the voice and actor on film; which is what he was doing at the present moment. It seemed ironical that such a signal honour should come from France, and not his own country . . . however; Resnais did so.

The troupe left it to me to ask him to speak these lines on to the tape and dispatched me across the grassy terrace to where he was sitting doing *The Times* crossword. He heard me out politely and refused absolutely.

'But John, why? It's such a little thing.' I could see the troupe standing some way off watching me anxiously.

'My dear boy,' he said. '*I'm* not the star of the film. You are. It's your job.'

'You are the star, for God's sake.'

He looked up with a grin. 'You have top billing. So *you* are.'

I walked back to a saddened troupe. 'He won't.'

Their disappointment was so obvious, so dejected did they look, that I decided to go back and have another try. I knelt beside John's chair in my most supplicatory manner, and spoke to him in a low voice. For the troupe had inched nearer anxiously.

'Now, John, listen. They want Alain to hear your voice on the tape; for it to be the first sound recorded on the new machine. Their gift.'

He didn't even look up: shook his head, printed a word, deliberately, in the white spaces of his crossword.

I was desperate. 'John. Please. You probably have one of the most beautiful English-speaking voices in the world . . .'

He looked up over the top of his glasses. 'THE!' he said sharply. And spoke the message.

◊

Sir Alec Guinness's definition of Sir John's voice:
Like a silver trumpet muffled in silk.

◊

Sir Michael Redgrave:
We assembled for the first reading of *Richard II*. I felt proud to be a member of such a company: Gielgud as Richard; Peggy Ashcroft as the Queen; Leon Quatermaine as John of Gaunt; Frederick Lloyd; Harcourt Williams: Dorothy Green; beside them Anthony Quayle, Alec Guinness, Glen Byam Shaw, and George Devine. Gielgud himself was directing. He was only three or four years my senior, but I was still a comparative newcomer, with only three years' professional experience behind me; Gielgud had been a leading actor for more than a decade . . . It was a nerve-wracking occasion. I raced through Bolingbroke's first speech without difficulty, but when I came to his entrance in the lists—'Harry of Hereford, Lancaster, and Derby am I'—I tripped over my tongue, pronounced 'Hereford' as 'Hertford', and came to a halt. 'That was wrong,

wasn't it?' 'Quite wrong,' said John, smiling. I took a deep breath and began again.

John, even at the first reading, was as near perfect as I could wish or imagine. Ninety per cent of the beauty of his acting was the beauty of his voice. To this day I can see no way of improving on the dazzling virtuosity of phrasing and breathing which was Gielgud's in the cadenza beginning:

Draw near,
And list what with our council we have done.

◊

Clive Hodgson on Sir John:
If all art aspires to the condition of music, then no one has done more to realize the aspirations of the art of acting.

◊

John Mortimer:
Like all great original artists Gielgud's influence spread far beyond his own particular art. My father relied on the Gielgud *vox humana* in all his speeches in Probate actions, and I still hear echoes of it when making a final appeal to the jury. So what started in the great days of the Old Vic with a young, awkward actor whose one lugubrious line was, 'Here is the number of the slaughtered French,' can end up extremely usefully in a murder case down at the Old Bailey. However poor the imitation, the effect still appears to enthrall the jury.

◊

Sir John recalls advice given to him by Mrs Patrick Campbell during a rehearsal for *Ghosts*, which was being produced to commemorate the Ibsen centenary in 1927:

In the scene where Oswald tells his mother of his terrible disease, she said: 'Keep still. Gaze at me. Now, you must speak in a Channel-steamer voice. Empty your voice of meaning and speak as if you were going to be sick. Pinero once told me this and I have never forgotten it.'

◊

James Agate's opinion of the voice:
His grace and his poise are remarkable and his voice would melt the entire Inland Revenue.

◊

Judi Dench:
Hearing John do a sonnet, you get those fourteen lines, and it's as though they've been wrapped at Fortnum's. Not that it's just glitter; for John can present an entirety of something. Maybe because of that musicality of his voice, but that's certainly not to negate his intellect.

◊

Lord Olivier's definition:
The voice that wooed the world.

◊

Angus McBean:
Every year I used to go to the Old Vic Ball which was usually on the stage at the Lyceum, as I remember it. It was mainly to dress up, which I have always loved, and one year, having won the first prize for my costume, I

78

found that John was giving away the prizes and heard that extraordinary, idiosyncratic and quite beautiful voice saying, 'What an extraordinary costume—but, dear boy, I'm deeply embarrassed to have to give you this.' This was a set of records of him orating Shakespeare's most famous soliloquies: heavy, twelve-inch, single-sided 78s; to me the greatest joy.

◊

Judi Dench;

The wonderful thing about John Gielgud and Frank Sinatra, from a student's point of view, is that John, like Sinatra, presents the entire arc of meaning of a soliloquy in the way Sinatra does with a song. When John reads a sonnet, he doesn't run out of breath after the first line. You know, you get some actors who will go, 'TO—BE—OR—NOT—TO—BE.' Over explanatory. 'IF—'TWERE—DONE—WHEN—'TIS—DONE.' Somehow, John Gielgud sees the sphere of the things he's saying, like Frank Sinatra singing a song. He is able to carry lots of threads of meaning. He is the Sinatra of verse-speaking.

◊

Lord Olivier remembers his first acting partnership with Sir John. In *Romeo and Juliet*, they alternated the playing of Romeo and Mercutio:

It's very easy, looking back, to criticize, but in those days there was a way of doing things. That's how they were *done*, and that's what the public came to see. They wanted their verse spoken beautifully, and if that was not how you delivered it, you were considered as upstart, an outsider. So I was the outsider and John was the jewel; and a shining one too, deservedly so. John still has the most beautiful voice, but I felt in

79

those days he allowed it to dominate his performances and, if he was lost but for a moment, he would dive straight back into its honey.

The Critics

Sir John on the criticism of Kenneth Tynan:
It's wonderful when it isn't you.

◊

Kenneth Tynan writing about Sir John's performance in Graham Greene's *The Potting Shed*, at the Globe
Theatre, 1958:
Very wrought-up he was, very curt and brusque—
you know how he used to talk to other actors as if he
was going to tip them?

◊

John Mortimer recalls lunch with Sir John. Once
again, the problem of critics recurred:
When I last enjoyed lunch with him he talked, as
usual, incessantly with hardly a pause for breath. His
eyes turned to gaze about the room as though through
modesty, not wishing to take part in the conversation.
His hands moved rhythmically and he said, 'Tynan said

I had only two gestures, the left hand up, the right hand up. What did he want me to do, bring out my prick?'

◊

Herbert Farjeon writing about a production of *The Three Sisters* of 1937 which starred Sir John:

It is in the order of things that a critic should praise this play. It is in the order of things that an audience, to signify appreciation, should applaud it. Yet one praises and applauds with reluctance. Silence is the perfectest herald of joy. One is so overwhelmed by the poignant beauty of the production that anything written or spoken must fall far short of what one feels. Moreover, the emotional reaction is so personal, so private, that one is in no mood for eloquence . . . There is a tenderness in the acting so exquisite that it is like the passing of light.

◊

Sir John:
James Agate was very kind and sympathetic to me.

◊

James Agate:
Mr Gielgud is becoming one of our most admirable actors: there is mind behind everything he does. Only he must avoid the snag of portentousness, of being intense about nothing in particular.

◊

Kenneth Tynan reviewed *Venice Preserv'd* at the Lyric, Hammersmith, 1953:
The play's major flaw is that Otway allows Jaffeir far

too much self-pity, a mood of which John Gielgud, as an actor, is far too fond. The temptation sometimes proves too much for him: inhaling passionately through the nose, he administers to every line a tremendous parsonical quiver. But pictorially, if not emotionally, this is a very satisfying performance.

♦

Michael Coveney:
Richardson's idiosyncratic dapperness seems always to be a consciously cultivated characteristic, whereas Gielgud effortlessly emanates style, polish, assurance. You see old men like Richardson walking briskly along the seafront in Eastbourne or Hove. But you cannot put a postmark on Gielgud's brand of seigneurial old age. The wonderful paradox is that Gielgud, a monarch in exile from a distant theatrical and social élite, is ideally and mysteriously equipped to play the role of an aloof participant in the suburban meanderings of a theatre that both adores and mistrusts him.

♦

When Sir John invited Lord Olivier to join his production of *Romeo and Juliet* in 1935 with a view to their alternating the roles of Romeo and Mercutio, Charles Morgan wrote in *The Times*: When Mr Gielgud played Mercutio he gave us the cascade but failed at the bluff. There is plenty of honest rock about Mr Olivier's Mercutio, though he turns on the poetry in the way that athletic young fellows turn on the morning bath.

♦

Ivor Brown, describing Gielgud in his first *Romeo* at the Regent, London, 1924:

The most meaningless legs imaginable.

◊

Kenneth Tynan reviewing *The Ages of Man* at the 46th Street Theatre, New York:

I have always felt that Sir John Gielgud is the finest actor on earth from the neck up . . . Poker-backed he may be, poker-faced he certainly isn't. Wherever pride, scorn, compassion, and more cerebral kinds of agony are called for, his features respond promptly, and memorably.

◊

The verdict on Sir John's legs seemed to be unanimous. Another judgement, from 1922:

Mr Gielgud from the waist downwards means absolutely nothing. He has the most meaningless legs imaginable.

◊

There was a time when Sir John was judged incapable of acting in contemporary drama.

James Agate on a melodrama called *Katerina*:

Twice in this play he has to make an entry upstairs from below stage. The first time is an occasion of great solemnity, but on the second he is merely paying a friendly call to do which it is unnecessary to put on the manner of one rising from the grave.

◊

Kenneth Tynan was similarly uneasy with Gielgud's presence in modern drama. Of Sir John's performance in Noel Coward's *Nude With Violin* of 1955, he wrote:

Sir John never acts seriously in modern dress; it is the lounging attire in which he relaxes between classical bookings; and his present performance as a simpering valet is an act of boyish mischief, carried out with extreme elegance and the general aspect of a tight, smart, walking umbrella.

◊

Sir John:
One afternoon, the famous critic, James Agate, bustled into my dressing-room half-way through the matinée performance (of *Macbeth*, in 1929) . . . He began by saying that he had dragged himself to the theatre full of the direst presentiments; that I should fail as Macbeth had seemed a foregone conclusion to him. He then remarked: 'I have never seen the Murder Scene better done, and so I have come to congratulate you now. At the end of the performance I shall probably have changed my mind, for you can't possibly play the rest of it.' . . . I was amazed to read a favourable notice in his column the following Sunday.

◊

Kenneth Tynan:
Sir John Gielgud is far greater than the sum of his parts.

◊

James Harding was James Agate's biographer. It is not always easy defending one's biographical subject:
Gielgud and Agate lunched together at the Ivy on

alternate Mondays, paying for the meal, at Agate's suggestion, on equal terms. One day Gielgud bought him a bottle of champagne. The following week Agate returned the compliment with a miserly glass of lemonade. He was full of advice, often delivered in a curiously brutal and insensitive way.

◊

Sir John:
One morning I approached Emlyn Williams a little nervously and said that I thought an opening scene was unduly encumbered with the names of flowers. Would he agree to my making a few cuts, as these repeated floral allusions rather held up the action? 'By all means,' said Emlyn. 'We don't want James Agate to head his Sunday article, "Herrick, or Little by Little".'

◊

Tynan reviewed Sir John's *Hamlet* of 1944 at the Haymarket:
Body and soul seem always to be at odds in John Gielgud's work . . . His voice is all soul, injured and struggling: but the body is curiously ineffectual, with the result, for me, that his acting lacks stomach and heart. He prances fluently enough, but with the grace of ballet rather than animals and men. One thinks of Olivier in terms of other species, of panthers and lions: one thinks of Gielgud in terms of other arts, of ballet and portrait painting.
His face is best in repose: in the eyes there is noble rebuke, in the pursed lips and sunk cheeks you discern a defiant melancholy, overcast by wisdom and the traditional poet's sadness. The voice is thrilling and bears witness to great suffering: an East wind has blown through it.

◊

86

Thirty-odd years later, it was the voice that critics were still praising above all else, at least where Sir John's classical roles were concerned. Michael Billington:

I was never quite persuaded by him as the eponymous hero in a National Theatre version of *Julius Caesar*. He phrased the part with impeccable intelligence . . . but he struck me as a singularly beneficent ruler rather than an overweening tyrant and the result was to make the conspiracy look like a gratuitous attempt to kill off the best verse speaker on the English stage.

ǫ

Kenneth Tynan:

There is, you see, a gulf fixed between good and great performances; but a bridge spans it, over which you may stroll if your visa is in order. Mr Redgrave, ignoring this, always chooses the hard way. He dives into the torrent and tries to swim across, usually sinking within sight of the shore. Olivier pole-vaults over in a single animal leap; Gielgud, seizing a parasol, crosses by tight-rope; Redgrave alone must battle it out with the current. The ensuing spectacle is never dull, but it can be very painful to watch.

ǫ

Sir John:

I never feel at ease if a critic comes to my dressing-room. Critics, like clergymen, always seem out of place behind the scenes!

ǫ

Kenneth Tynan:

Gielgud is an actor who refuses to compromise with

his audience: he does not offer a welcoming hand, but binds a spell instead. They must accept him on his own intellectual level, or not at all . . . The contrast between Gielgud and Olivier is instructive . . . For the large, shattering effects of passion, we look to Olivier; for the smaller, more exquisite effects of temper, to Gielgud. To use an old and respectable critical terminology, it is the contrast between Nature and Art.

Sir John as a Brick-dropper

Harold Hobson:
Sir John is the man 'who has brought the art of the impishly desired involuntary *gaffe* to its highest peak of perfection'.

◊

Sir John:
I seem in my time to have dropped enough bricks to build a new Wall of China.

◊

Sir Alec Guinness's early impression of Sir John:
There was nothing he lacked, as far as I could see, except tact. His tactless remarks, over the decades, have joined the ranks of the happiest theatre legends of our time and, apart from their sheer funniness, they have always been entirely forgivable because they spring spontaneously from the heart without a glimmer of malice.

Peter Sallis:

Straight from the Royal Academy of Dramatic Art, I was awarded the Tennent contract at twelve pounds a week. At my first interview with John Perry and the crowned heads, John Gielgud explained in three minutes how he intended to produce *Richard II* and asked what I would like to play. There seemed only one part for me and I opted for the gardener. 'That's cast,' Gielgud told me. Then turning to the others, 'He might be Green, he might be Green!' Then turning back to me he explained kindly, 'We've two men playing Bushy and Baghot, very beautiful, you might make a good contrast.'

Finally cast as Lord Ross or something equally obscure, at the read-through I sat in the rear rank behind Paul Scofield, Joy Parker, Herbert Lomas, Veronica Turnleigh, Richard Wordsworth and all. After the read-through Gielgud offered his congratulations to the cast, adding, 'There's only one voice that is wrong, and that is,' he considers his list, 'Peter Sallis. What are you playing?'

'Lord Ross,' I explained meekly.

'How would you like to play servant to the Duke of York?'

Later he probably had to tell this to John Perry, who must have pointed out that Sallis was being paid twelve pounds a week, a princely sum in those days, and they could get anyone off the street to play servant to the Duke of York for eight pounds. When Gielgud started to set the play and it came to my entrance, I had to utter the immortal line, 'An hour before I came the Duchess died,' and leave the stage.

Gielgud called me back: 'Peter, is that all you do?'

'Yes.'

'Oh Christ!'

I finally got to play the gardener, but not in that production, and I only mention it to give the story a happy ending.

Peter Ustinov:

I once saw Sir John on a local late-night television interview in Saint Louis, Missouri. He was busy playing *The Ages of Man*, his one-man show, in half a ball-park, and now he was being interviewed by a long-winded intellectual.

'One final question,' the interviewer said. 'Sir . . . Sir Gielgud . . . did you . . . oh, you must have had . . . we all did . . . at the very start of your very wonderful . . . very wonderful and very meaningful . . . let me put it this way . . . did you have someone . . . a man . . . or . . . indeed, a woman . . . at whom you could point a finger and say . . . Yes! . . . This person helped me when I . . .'

By now John understood what was being asked of him, and he prepared to answer, disguising his dislike of all that is pretentious by perfect courtesy.

'Yes, I think there was somebody who taught me a great deal at my dramatic school, and I certainly am grateful to him for his kindness and consideration towards me. His name was Claude Rains.'

And then, as an afterthought, he added—'I don't know what happened to him. I think he failed and went to America.'

◊

Emlyn Williams:

Edna Best was cast in *Spring, 1600* but early on in rehearsals, Williams recalls:

Next morning, on stage, John read a note from her: she suddenly had to leave for the States . . . 'It's Bart (Herbert Marshall, Best's husband), of course I did hear he's been a bit footloose in Hollywood.' It was not the happiest way to describe a glamorous film star who happened to be one-legged . . .

Michael Coveney:

My own especial favourite (brick) concerns a senior, rather dull supporting actor (now dead) whom we shall call 'Miles Thornton'. For weeks Thornton had been on tour with Gielgud and had received not one word, of abuse, encouragement or even greeting, from his by now terrifying colleague. Eventually the pressure was too much and the bemused thespian took his courage in both hands and, in one of the large provincial towns, stood trembling outside the Number One dressing-room. He knocked, tentatively, just before the half was called.

'Come,' cried Gielgud from within and, on seeing the vaguely familiar profile edging round the door, expostulated, 'My dear boy, thank heavens it's you. For one dreadful moment I thought it was going to be that ghastly old bore Miles Thornton.'

♭

Sir John:

I remember once making a *faux pas* with my cousin (Phyllis Neilson-Terry, with whom he was touring the provinces). I knew that she had first acted under the name of Phyllida Terson (a contraction of Terry and Neilson) and one night, trying to be funny, I knocked at her door and said, 'It's your call, Miss Terson.' She did not look at all pleased. I was told later that when she was called Phyllida Terson and acting with Herbert Tree, my aunt Marion, who was in the stalls, overheard somebody in the next seat saying, 'Of course, she's one of Tree's illegitimate children,' so she quickly changed her acting name to Neilson-Terry. I had no idea of the gaffe which I was committing (I have become famous for dropping similar bricks), but I tried to learn to behave more carefully . . .

Jeremy Irons:

I first met Sir John at Castle Howard in Yorkshire and spent seven happy days shooting with him for *Brideshead Revisited*. During our dinners together I relished his well-known brick-dropping and wickedness about some of the people he had worked with. When I mentioned that I found his dinner conversation more interesting and spicy than his recently-published autobiography, he said words to the effect of 'but of course I could not write that about them, some of them are still alive and they would be terribly upset'. What a shame autobiographies must necessarily be sanitized.

◊

Sir John Mills:

John Gielgud has a wonderful sense of humour, and is famous for dropping the most marvellous clangers. My favourite moment was during the dress rehearsal at the Haymarket Theatre. Some plays are absolutely hellish to rehearse. *Charley's Aunt* is one of them: without an audience it seems to be just about the un-funniest piece ever written. I finished the first act pouring with sweat after tearing round the stage in the heavy black frock, wig and bonnet. Johnny G. was out front in the stalls. There was dead silence. I walked to the footlights and, shading my eyes from the glare, peered out into the auditorium. 'Johnny,' I said, 'are you there?'

'Yes, I am.'

'Well . . . what did you think of it?'

'Interminable, my dear fellow, absolutely interminable.'

◊

Sir John:

After seeing Richard Burton's *Hamlet* when Burton

announced that he was suffering from a cold: 'I'll come back when you're better . . . in health I mean, of course.'

◊

Jack Hawkins:
I first worked with John Gielgud in his production of *Richard of Bordeaux*, when I took over the part of the Earl of Oxford from Francis Lister. A few months after I joined, the production celebrated its first anniversary, and of course there were a large number of *aficionados* at the front of the house.

At the end of the performance there were cries of 'Speech, speech!' and Johnny stepped forward. He thanked the audience for its support and said: 'I know that many of you have been to see us thirty or forty times.' He paused, and looked along the line of the cast, searching for words. His eyes lighted on me, and he added: 'In spite of the changes in the cast.'

◊

Stuart Burge:
When John Gielgud was visiting Nottingham in *Veterans* by Charles Wood, he used sometimes to frequent the stalls during my production of *The Tempest* starring Hugh Griffiths. Sir John was troubled at the time by a somewhat hostile reaction to his own play, so I decided to ask him to a supper party, also inviting Hugh Griffiths along. The subject of *The Tempest* came up and Sir John kept everyone, or nearly everyone, amused by his comments on previous productions he had witnessed. Apparently he had not been impressed by the Prospero and he held forth for some time as to the hopeless performance of Caliban in the same production. Then

glancing at Hugh Griffiths at the other end of the table, 'You're very silent, Hugh.'

'Not as a rule,' said Hugh. 'I was just trying to recall my performance and wondering if you could possibly be right.'

ϱ

Ned Sherrin:
When Sir Donald Wolfit died . . . I mounted his obituary programme at the BBC . . . I started to search for people to talk about Wolfit. It was important that it should be considered, but not solemn . . . First I looked for other knights who would speak of their peer. I did not approach Sir Ralph Richardson, understanding that there had been some friction long ago when they had both learned their business in a touring company run by an old actor-manager called Charles Doran . . . I tried Sir Laurence Olivier. But he was to read the lesson at the memorial service and thought that was enough. Sir Michael Redgrave was ill. Sir Alec Guinness's refusal was subtly judged: 'I thought he was a wonderful film actor,' he said. 'I never really saw him much in the theatre.' Finally I went down to the Old Vic to see Sir John Gielgud between performances—without much confidence. He was disarmingly frank as usual. 'I couldn't do it,' he said. 'It would be so hypocritical. We used to think he was a joke.'

ϱ

Sir John:
When Clement Attlee was Prime Minister, I was asked to meet him at Stratford-upon-Avon at a supper at the Falcon Hotel after he had attended a performance (one I was not in myself). I sat next to his daughter and the conversation turned on where we lived.

'I have a very convenient home in Westminster,' I remarked. 'So easy to walk to the theatre. And where do you live?'

Miss Attlee looked distinctly surprised and replied curtly, 'Number Ten, Downing Street.'

♩

Sir Alec Guinness:
When I was beginning to play leading roles, he stopped me one day in Piccadilly, saying, 'I can't think why you want to play big parts. Why don't you stick to the little people you do so well?' 'I wasn't awfully good as the Groom in *Richard II*,' I said. 'No. I suppose you weren't.' 'And I was even worse as Ammerle.' 'Possibly. Shall we go and see a flick?'

♩

Sir Cecil Beaton:
A man called on Sir John Gielgud in his dressing-room at the theatre to congratulate him on his performance.

Sir John said, 'How pleased I am to meet you. I used to know your son, we were at school together.'

The man replied, 'I have no son, I was at school with you.'

♩

Emlyn Williams:
Early in the Gielgud career, at the Ivy Restaurant, he was the luncheon guest of a prominent playwright of the time who was notoriously dull and garrulous company. Just as there came a pause for breath, a man passed the table. 'Thank God he didn't stop,' said John,

'he's a bigger bore than Eddie Knoblock,' and turned back to his host. Who was Eddie Knoblock . . .

◊

Dame Peggy Ashcroft:
John Gielgud, after his first ever production, *Romeo and Juliet*, for the OUDS in 1932, in his curtain speech, holding Edith Evans and myself by the hand, said, 'I hope never to have two such leading ladies again.'

◊

Paul Scofield:
Paul Scofield regards Sir John as the 'prototype brick-dropper' and recalls a dress rehearsal of Sir John's production of a Mozart opera at Covent Garden when something went wrong on stage: 'Oh stop, stop, stop! Do stop that *dreadful* music!'

◊

Michael Coveney:
If I do Sir John a disservice I can only claim in my defence that many of *his* stories, delightedly recounted in legend and in print, are equally apocryphal. I have had occasion to check one or two about Ingrid Bergman ('Dear Ingrid—speaks five languages and can't act in any of them') and find them rooted in fact but flamboyantly elaborated for effect.

◊

Emlyn Williams:
John was casting *The Laughing Woman*, a play about a brilliant young sculptor and his mistress. 'Bronnie is insisting on Stephen Haggard for the part. He's splendid

but *much* too well-bred. It calls for an actor who would convey somebody savage, uncouth—Emlyn, *you* should be playing it!'

◊

Emlyn Williams:

In 1940, again at the Old Vic, and again a curtain speech, after a performance of *The Tempest*, I was in the audience. It was at one of the darkest moments of the war . . . many mothers with American connections had decided to brave the very real submarine dangers of the Atlantic and set out with their small children. One of their number was Jessica Tandy, who had opened as Miranda, played until she sailed, and was then replaced by Peggy Ashcroft . . . After this particular performance Prospero stepped forward and held out a hand to stem the applause. 'Ladies and gentlemen, I know you will rejoice with all of us, in relief at the news just received—Jessica Tandy is safely in America!'

It seemed to me that for a second Peggy was wondering how to make clear that she was showing the right kind of relief, adds Williams.

◊

Emlyn Williams again:

In 1933, during the run of *Richard of Bordeaux*, he directed *The Merchant of Venice* at the Old Vic. During the rehearsals necessary during his performances at the New, he was helped out by Harcourt Williams, the distinguished veteran actor-director whom he much admired. Nobody could have appreciated the gesture more than John. Came the first night. At the end of his performance at the New, John scrambled out of his clothes and into a taxi, and got to the Old Vic in time for the last curtain. At the end of the calls, and the

98

cheers, he joined the actors, praised and thanked them all beautifully, and finished up with, 'The person to whom I am truly grateful is my friend Harcourt Williams, who has—believe me—done all the donkey-work.'

Sir John the Joker

Judi Dench:
I quickly realized, working with John, that he is a
terrible corpser, a really bad laugher. Leslie Banks was
the worst, the very worst. Then it goes John, and then
Laurence Olivier, and, then a jump to Kenneth
Branagh. I'm somewhere in there. I thought I was the
worst till I met Ken Branagh. And Michael Gambon:
there's a league of us.

$\natural$

Sir John seems to have had a somewhat risqué sense
of humour from his earliest days in the theatre.
Emlyn Williams recalls him as a star of the OUDS in
the Twenties, when it was customary for the principal
Oxford dramatic society to invite London stars to head
each season, rather than relying on the attributes of the
undergraduates. Just as you were envying the poise and
the swift unequivocal judgement—on Ibsen, Shakespearean obscurities, Purcell's theatre music, Shaw's
impending *Saint Joan*, Edith Evans' Millamant, Stanis-

lavsky—with every comment irradiated by a passionate interest in people and things which made his conversation quite free from self-display; just as you sat increasingly in awe of the imperious turn of the head, the pundit would toss into the air some appetizing morsel of trivial West End gossip, embellished with some atrociously risqué pun—'This Tallulah is *too* much, in *The Dancers*! Apparently she wears not a stitch underneath, a case of no drawers makes you a draw I suppose, not beating about the bush when *she* does a high kick!—and then a shrill cackle utterly at variance with the other personality.

♀

Judi Dench:
I remember John in *The Cherry Orchard* with Patience Collyer. Just before we were due to go on for some scene or other, John handed Patience a cucumber and said 'Patience, put that somewhere for me will you?' Then he swept on as Gaev, with tears streaming down his face, leaving everyone in the wings uncontrollable with laughter.

♀

Sir Alec Guinness:
Three years ago, while being made up for a film I was doing in New York, the very jolly make-up artist said, 'Know any good limericks?' 'Very few.' I replied. 'When I used to make up Sir John Gielgud,' she went on, 'he used to tell me a dirty limerick every morning.' She fell about laughing at the recollection. What with *The Times* crossword and limericks he obviously begins each day with much mental activity, while most of us are still rubbing the sleep from our eyes.

Irene Worth:

Sir John is Shakespeare's brother in his love of puns . . . At the dress rehearsal of *Oedipus* . . . I was to expire on this golden spike in a metaphor which involved horrendous gymnastics, more arduous, it seemed to me, than anything demanded even of dancers.

'How is it?' called Peter (Brook, the director).

'A bit short,' I called back.

'Sorry,' said Peter. 'What can we do about that?'

'Well,' I pondered, 'perhaps we need a plinth!'

'Plinth Philip or Plinth Charles?' came from John in the wings, doubled up with laughter.

◊

Irene Worth again!

I had a walk-on part as a lady-in-waiting in *Henry VIII* at the Old Vic and John was playing Wolsey. And he used to come on each night with a different make-up. Then, suddenly, one night he came on with spots all over his face. 'My God, John!' I said. 'Yes, I've got frightfully bad skin!' he replied. It was terribly funny. And one night he came on just holding a carnation.

◊

Sir John on his involvement in a forgotten Napoleonic film, called *Eagle in a Cage*, which entailed many perilous ascents of a particularly craggy rock-face: *Climb and Punishment.*

◊

Michael Williams was also working on *Eagle in a Cage*:

I appeared in *Eagle in a Cage* with Kenneth Haigh, Billie Whitelaw, John and Ralph. It must be about eighteen years ago now. Ken and I had to ride two terrifying stallions. We all had dinner with John on the night that he came out to Yugoslavia to shoot his scenes. We'd already been thrown by them during rehearsals that day and the matter was duly discussed at dinner. The following morning John swept into the location dressing-room and said, 'I've just seen your two horses outside. I've decided to call them The Bolting Brothers.'

◊

Judi Dench:
I remember, during *The Cherry Orchard*, reading notices for John's Gaev. Generally, it was thought his performance was supreme. But one critic said, 'There is only one reservation I have, and that is that Gielgud did not seem to be enjoying eating the caramels as much as he should have'. And I thought, if John's read that, tomorrow night he's going to be unbelievable. When it came to the next night, he started *stuffing* himself *and* enjoying it. And then he dried on line and just started crying with laughter and said 'I'm so glad you, Leslie Banks and I aren't on stage together.'

◊

Emlyn Williams:
Without warning, the eyes fixed me like a searchlight. 'I loved your play (*Spring, 1600*). How do you feel about the last act? . . . Peggy (Ashcroft) for the girl, do you think? What about Edna (Best)? She was beastly to me in *The Nymph* but she has quality. Then there's Angela (Baddeley). She wouldn't play it Baddeley but Edna might be Best.'

◊

Richard Pasco:
Whilst a student at Central School in the summer of 1948 and taking part with other students (Barbara Jefford, amongst them) in the annual Ellen Terry Memorial Performance at the Barn Theatre in Tenterden, Kent, we as students dressed in cottages in the village. On going to rehearsal one morning we saw coming towards us an immaculately dark-suited Sir John. Seeing our student-like gazes and nudges of awe, as he approached he countered with, 'Ah, my dears, are you all full of the most *exquisite* nerves?'

ℓ

Judi Dench:
Someone told me a story about a group of actors, all of whom, apart from Sir John, will remain nameless, who were sitting around waiting for a shot to be lined up. Suddenly, this sublime voice began, 'Loveliest of trees/The cherry now', then somebody else took it up, then someone else the next line and so on until it got back to John for the last lines. 'And since to look at things in bloom/Forty years is little room/About the woodlands I will go/To see the cherry hung with snow/Don't you think that that Joe Bloggs is the most frightfully, crashingly boringly incompetent actor?'
And it was all done in one exquisite breath.

ℓ

Alan Bennett, during the preparations for *Forty Years On*:
A second meeting with Gielgud, lunch at the Ivy . . . more stories. Of Emerald Cunard, who summoned him to dine at the Dorchester during the Blitz. 'And a very dull meal it was, chicken and ice cream. Emerald surveyed the table and rang for the butler. 'And where is

the butter?' 'There is no butter, ma'am.' 'No butter? But what is the merchant navy doing?'

$$\diamond$$

Judi Dench:
I last saw John when we were both having fittings. I can't remember what he was being measured for, but I was being fitted for *Ghosts*. He said, 'Oh, Judi, what are you doing?' I said 'I'm playing Mrs Alby.' 'Oh, you're playing all the great parts. Judi. How does it happen? How do you get all those parts? I'm going off to do a film where I have to enter the gas chambers naked from behind.'

The Name and the Family

Advice to Sir John from an acting Terry:
You must never say it is a bad audience. It is your business to make it a good one.

ϙ

Sir John dwells on his second most famous attribute:
Possibly because I have a big nose, some people think that I have Jewish blood and am perfect for Jewish parts. I always rather hoped this was so because so many of the best actors in the world are Jewish. But I asked my father and he assured me that there is no Jewish blood in our family at all.

ϙ

Sir John:
Our name is Lithuanian—not Scottish, as many people imagine. It lends itself to an amazing variety of mispronunciations and strange spellings. (My mother once had a letter addressed to Mrs Gradgrind.)

Emlyn Williams:

On Monday evening, January 28th, 1924, when I was an undergraduate of eighteen and a bit, I sat in the Oxford Playhouse, then a flimsy sketchily converted building in the Woodstock Road. I was in my weekly (creaky) kitchen chair for the first night of Congreve's *Love for Love*. It was also the first appearance of a newcomer to the company. *Valentine* . . . John Gielgud.

Not knowing the play, I visualized him as a seasoned old character actor, fortyish. A woman behind me looked up from her programme and whispered, 'Poor man, how does he pronounce it, *Jeel*-gud?' It did look outlandish. Not a good stage name. I thought. As bad, in its way, as *Coward*. (John was to tell me, much later, that during his first job, on tour, the local paper had announced that 'the small part of the messenger was adequately portrayed by Joan Gillseed . . .')

The curtains parted to reveal Valentine seated at a table, reading and Jeel-gud turned out to be young (not yet twenty) and very striking in a long curly wig. He motioned languidly to his servant. 'Jeremy, take this book away. I'll take a turn and digest what I've read.'

To begin with, the usual creaking; but once he got going, in his first leading part, all nose and passion and dragging calves and unbridled oboe of a voice—how nervous he must have been—the creaking stopped. It was all a little large for the hall, but the tall haughty creature held the stage all right, and went mad with a will. Later in the week, *Isis* couldn't get his name right either. 'A very interesting performance by Mr Gielgerd.'

§

This was not the first time that Sir John's name had attracted comment, as he himself recalls:

I also played the opening scene of Hotspur, from

Henry IV, Part I, for a diploma competition (while at RADA, 1921–1922), and was complimented by the judges. Next day, one of them sent me a charming letter of congratulation and summoned me to his office, where he spent half an hour sipping a glass of milk and begging me to change my name for the stage, as no one would ever be able to spell or pronounce it properly. I answered obstinately that if anyone did notice it they would not easily forget it, and so we parted.

ϕ

Lindsay Anderson:

As I observed often in the theatre, Gielgud has a natural artistic aristocracy which transforms him, in that split second when he steps from the wings on to the stage, from a charming, loquacious man into a great actor of effortless stature. This it is to be a Terry.

ϕ

Sir John describes the great acting dynasty of which he is a member:

As a family the Terrys have not a great sense of humour.

A matter to be disputed!

Bibliography

Sir Peter Hall's Diaries: The story of a dramatic battle.
Hamish Hamilton, 1983.

A View of the English Stage by Kenneth Tynan.
Methuen, 1975.

The West End – Mismanagement and Snobbery by
John Picks.

These Our Actors by Richard Findlater.
Hamish Hamilton, 1983.

John Gielgud: A Celebration by Gyles Brandreth.
Pavilion Books, 1985.

An Orderly Man by Dirk Bogarde.
Chatto and Windus, 1983.

The Ages of Gielgud – An Actor at Eighty ed. Ronald
Harwood.
Hodder and Stoughton, 1984.

An Actor and His Time by John Gielgud.
Sidgwick and Jackson, 1979.

Robert Morley's Book of Bricks.
Weidenfeld and Nicolson, 1978.

The History of the National Theatre by John Elsom and Nicholas Tomalin.
Jonathan Cape, 1978.

Early Stages by John Gielgud.
Heinemann, 1939.

Ralph Richardson: An Actor's Life by Gary O'Connor.
Hodder and Stoughton, 1982.

Olivier: In Celebration ed. Gary O'Connor.
Hodder and Stoughton, 1987.

The Life of Kenneth Tynan by Kathleen Tynan.
Weidenfeld and Nicolson, 1987.

Confessions of an Actor by Laurence Olivier.
Weidenfeld and Nicolson, 1982.

Up in the Clouds, Gentlemen Please by Sir John Mills.

Anything for a Quite Life. The Autobiography of Jack Hawkins.

In My Mind's Eye. The Autobiography of Sir Michael Redgrave.
Hodder and Stoughton, 1984.

A Small Thing – Like An Earthquake. The Autobiography of Ned Sherrin.

Blessings in Disguise. The Autobiography of Sir Alec Guinness.
Hamish Hamilton, 1985.

The Everyman Book of Theatrical Anecdotes ed. Donald Sinden.

A Touch of the Memoirs by Donald Sinden.
Hodder and Stoughton, 1982.

On Acting by Laurence Olivier.

Agate: A Biography by James Harding.